THE SOUL OF TH[illegible]TTE

John Gray is the author of a number of highly regarded and controversial books, including *False Dawn*, *Straw Dogs* and, most recently, *The Silence of Animals*. He has taught at Oxford, Harvard, Yale and the LSE. John Banville described *The Silence of Animals* as 'a marvellous statement of what it is to be both an animal and a human in the strange, terrifying and exquisite world in which we straw dogs find ourselves'.

JOHN GRAY

The Soul of the Marionette

A Short Enquiry into Human Freedom

PENGUIN BOOKS

PENGUIN BOOKS

UK | USA | Canada | Ireland | Australia
India | New Zealand | South Africa

Penguin Books is part of the Penguin Random House group of companies
whose addresses can be found at global.penguinrandomhouse.com.

First published by Allen Lane 2015
Published in Penguin Books 2016
002

Typeset by Palimpsest Book Production Ltd, Falkirk, Stirlingshire
Printed in Great Britain by Clays Ltd, St Ives plc

A CIP catalogue record for this book is available from the British Library

978–0–241–95390–7

. . . grace will be most purely present in the human frame that either has no consciousness or an infinite amount of it, which is to say either in a marionette or in a god.

Heinrich von Kleist, 'The Puppet Theatre'

I mean, after all: you have to consider we're only made out of dust.

Philip K. Dick, *The Three Stigmata of Palmer Eldritch*

Contents

1 The Faith of Puppets

In the first centuries of our era, the Gnostics disputed with the Christians. They were annihilated, but we can imagine their possible victory.

Jorge Luis Borges, 'A Defense of Basilides the False'

THE FREEDOM OF THE MARIONETTE

A puppet may seem the embodiment of a lack of freedom. Whether moved by a hidden hand or pulled about by strings, a puppet has no will of its own. All of its movements are directed by the will of another – a human being who has decided what the puppet will do. Entirely controlled by a mind outside itself, a puppet has no choice in how it lives.

This would be an unbearable situation, if it were not for the fact that a puppet is an inanimate object. In order to feel a lack of freedom you must be a self-conscious being. But a puppet is a thing of wood and cloth, a human artefact without feeling or consciousness. A puppet has no soul. As a result, it cannot know it is unfree.

For Heinrich von Kleist, on the other hand, puppets represented a kind of freedom that human beings would never achieve. In his essay 'The Puppet Theatre', first published in 1810, the German writer has the narrator, wandering through a city park, meeting 'Herr C.', the recently appointed first dancer at the Opera. Noticing him on several occasions at a puppet theatre that had been erected in the town's market square, the narrator expresses surprise that a dancer should attend such 'little burlesques'.

Replying, Herr C. suggests that a dancer could learn a great deal from these puppet shows. Aren't marionettes – controlled from above by puppeteers – often extremely graceful in their movements as they dance? No human being can match the marionette in effortless grace. The puppet is:

> incapable of *affectation*. – For affectation occurs, as you know, whenever the soul . . . is situated in a place other than a movement's centre of gravity. Since the puppeteer, handling the wire or the string, can have no point except that one under his control, all the other limbs are what they should be: dead, mere pendula, and simply obey the law of gravity; an excellent attribute that you will look for in vain among the majority

> of our dancers . . . these puppets have the advantage of being *resistant to gravity*. Of the heaviness of matter, the factor that most works against the dancer, they are entirely ignorant: because the force lifting them into the air is greater than the one attaching them to the earth . . . Marionettes only *glance* the ground, like elves, the momentary halt lends the limbs a new impetus; but we use it to *rest* on, to recover from the exertion of the dance: a moment which clearly is not dance at all in itself and which we can do nothing with except get it over with as quickly as possible.

When the narrator reacts with astonishment to these paradoxical assertions, Herr C., 'taking a pinch of snuff', remarks that he should read 'the third chapter of Genesis attentively'. The narrator grasps the point: he is 'perfectly well aware of the damage done by consciousness to the natural grace of a human being'. But still he is sceptical, so Herr C. tells him the story of how he had fenced with a bear. A practised swordsman, he could easily have pierced the heart of a human being; but the animal, seemingly without any effort, avoided any harm:

> Now I tried a thrust, now a feint, the sweat was dripping off me: all in vain! Not only did the bear, like the foremost fencer in the world, parry all my thrusts; when I feinted – no fencer in the world can follow

> him in this – he did not even react: looking me in the eye, as though he could read my soul in it, he stood with his paw lifted in readiness and when my thrusts were not seriously intended he did not move.

Humans cannot emulate the grace of such an animal. Neither the beast nor the puppet is cursed with self-reflective thought. That, as Kleist sees it, is why they are free. If humans can ever achieve such a state it will only be after a transmutation in which they become infinitely more conscious:

> just as two lines intersecting at a point after they have passed through an infinity will suddenly come together again on the other side, or the image in a concave mirror, after travelling away into infinity, suddenly comes close up to us again, so when consciousness has, as we might say, passed through an infinity, grace will return; so that grace will be most purely present in the human frame that has either no consciousness or an infinite amount of it, which is to say either in a marionette or in a god.

The dialogue concludes:

> 'But,' I said rather distractedly, 'should we have to eat again of the Tree of Knowledge to fall back into the state of innocence?'

'Indeed,' he replied; 'that is the final chapter in the history of the world.'

Kleist's essay was one of the last things he wrote. Born into the Prussian military caste in 1777, he was temperamentally unsuited to any kind of conventional career. Pressed by his family to join the civil service, he saw himself as a writer but struggled to produce anything that satisfied him, travelling here and there across Europe, burning what he had written. At one point, seeming to have given up the struggle, he attempted to join Napoleon's army as it was preparing to invade England. Undoubtedly a writer of genius, he left seven plays, eight extraordinary stories and a number of essays and letters, and may have written a novel he destroyed before committing suicide in 1811. Congenitally restless, he could not find a place in the world.

With its teasingly enigmatic dialogue, the essay upsets everything modern humankind believes about itself. How could a puppet – a mechanical device without any trace of conscious awareness – be freer than a human being? Is it not this very awareness that marks us off from the rest of the world and enables us to choose our own path in life? Yet as Kleist pictures it, the automatism of the puppet is far from being a condition of slavery. Compared with that of humans, the life of the marionette looks more like an enviable state of freedom.

The idea that self-awareness may be an obstacle to living in freedom is not new. It has long been suspected that the ordinary mode of consciousness leaves human beings stuck between the mechanical motions of the flesh and the freedom of the spirit. That is why, in mystical traditions throughout history, freedom has meant an inner condition in which normal consciousness has been transcended.

In modern thinking freedom is not much more than a relationship between human beings. Freedom in this sense may come in a number of varieties. There is the freedom that consists in an absence of human obstacles to doing what you want or may come to want, sometimes called negative freedom; the kind that implies not just an absence of impediments, but acting as a rational human being would act; and the sort that you exercise when you are a member of a community or a state that determines how it will be governed. For Kleist and others who have thought like him, however, freedom is not simply a relationship between human beings: it is, above all, a state of the soul in which conflict has been left behind.

In ancient Europe, Stoics asserted that a slave could be freer than a master who suffers from self-division. In China, Daoists imagined a type of sage who responded to the flow of events without weighing alternatives. Disciples of monotheistic faiths have believed something similar: freedom, they say, is obeying God's will. What those who follow these traditions want most is not any kind of freedom of choice. Instead, what they long for is freedom *from* choice.

It is easy to dismiss those who yearn for this freedom as wanting to be ruled by a tyrant. After all, that is what many human beings have wanted in the past and continue to want today. Wanting freedom to choose may be a universal impulse, but it is far from being the strongest. It is not just that there are many things human beings want before they want this freedom – such as food to eat and a place to live. More to the point, if freedom means letting others live as they please there will always be many who are happy to be without freedom themselves.

In contrast, those who seek inner freedom do not care what kind of government they live under as long as it does not prevent them from turning within themselves. This may seem a selfish attitude; but it makes sense in a time of endemic instability, when political systems cannot be expected to last. One such time was late European antiquity, when Christianity contended with Greco-Roman philosophies and mystery religions. Another may be today, when belief in political solutions is fading and renascent religion contends with the ruling faith in science.

In late antiquity it was accepted that freedom was not a condition that could be established among human beings; the world was too unruly. Some of the mystical currents at work at the time went further: freedom meant escaping from the world. When Herr C. tells the narrator that he should read the third chapter of Genesis, Kleist points towards the most radical of these traditions – the religion of Gnosticism.

In the Genesis myth Adam and Eve lived in the Garden of Eden having no need to work; but a serpent tempted them, promising that if they ate the forbidden apple of knowledge they would be like gods. They ate the apple. Having disobeyed God, they were punished by having to pass their lives in unending labour.

In a traditional reading eating the apple was the original sin; but, as Gnostics understood the story, the two primordial humans were right to eat the apple. The God that commanded them not to do so was not the true God but only a demiurge, a tyrannical underling exulting in its power, while the serpent came to free them from slavery. True, when they ate the apple Adam and Eve fell from grace. This was indeed the Fall of Man – a fall into the dim world of everyday consciousness. But the Fall need not be final. Having eaten its fill from the Tree of Knowledge, humankind can then rise into a state of conscious innocence. When this happens, Herr C. declares, it will be 'the final chapter in the history of the world'.

Herr C. invokes one of the most uncompromising demands for freedom that has ever been made. Believing humans were botched creations of a demiurge – a malign or incompetent deity, not the true God which has disappeared from the world – the ancient Gnostics viewed the experience of choosing as confirming that human beings are radically flawed. Real freedom would be a condition in which they would no longer labour under the burden of choice – a condition that could be attained only by exiting from the natural world. For these forgotten visionaries, freedom was achieved by storming the heavens in an act of metaphysical violence.

Many people today hold to a Gnostic view of things without realizing the fact. Believing that human beings can be fully understood in the terms of scientific materialism, they reject any idea of free will. But they cannot give up hope of being masters of their destiny. So they have come to believe that science will somehow enable the human mind to escape the limitations that shape its natural condition. Throughout much of the world, and particularly in western countries, the Gnostic faith that knowledge can give humans a freedom no other creature can possess has become the predominant religion.

If one of Kleist's marionettes were somehow to achieve self-awareness, Gnosticism would be its religion. In the most ambitious versions of scientific materialism, human beings *are* marionettes: puppets on genetic strings, which by an accident of evolution have become self-aware. Unknown to those who most ardently profess it, the boldest secular thinkers are possessed by a version of mystical religion. At present, Gnosticism is the faith of people who believe themselves to be machines.

THE FAITH OF PUPPETS

Going far back into the ancient world, recurring in cultures widely separated in space and time, surfacing in religion, philosophy and the occult, exercising a powerful influence in modern science and politics, Gnosticism has coexisted and competed with, secreted itself within and hidden itself from many other ways of thinking. There have been Gnostic strands in Judaism, Christianity and Islam, Zoroastrianism, Manichaeism, Mithraism and Orphism, while Gnostic ideas established a powerful presence in Greek philosophy among some of the later followers of Plato.

The origins of Gnosticism have not been traced, but it seems to have emerged as a fully fledged worldview around the same time as Christianity. Like other Jewish prophets of the time, Jesus may have been influenced by Zoroastrian traditions that understood human life in terms of a war between good and evil. Christianity – the religion conjured from Jesus' life and sayings by St Paul – always contained Gnostic currents, though these were condemned as heresies that threatened the authority of the Church.

Gnostic ideas are far from being distinctively modern, but they emerged in more overt forms with the rise of the Renaissance. Revered by rationalists as the time when classical civilization was rediscovered, this was a period in which belief in magic flourished at the highest levels of the state. Alchemists and spirit-seers were regularly consulted at the court of Elizabeth, and even as older forms of religion were abandoned new types of magic were spreading. The seventeenth-century German astrologer and astronomer, mathematician and mystic Johannes Kepler is an emblematic Renaissance figure. While he believed in a cosmos governed by principles of order and harmony, Kepler set in motion a shift towards a world-view in which any laws that existed in the universe were mechanical and devoid of purpose. Other early modern scientists were similarly ambiguous. Isaac Newton was the founder of modern physics, but he was also a believer in alchemy and numerology and searched the apocalyptic books of the Bible for hidden meaning. The scientific revolution was, in many ways, a by-product of mysticism and magic. In fact, once the tangled origins of modern science are unravelled, it is doubtful whether a 'scientific revolution' occurred.

The novelist and poet Lawrence Durrell presented a modern version of the Gnostic vision in a series of novels, *The Avignon Quintet* (1974–85). Akkad, an Egyptian merchant-banker who is also a latter-day Gnostic, preaches to small groups of European expatriates. At times plump and sluggish-looking, at others looking ascetic and haggard, at home in four capitals and speaking as many languages or more, sometimes wearing western clothes and sometimes traditional dress, Akkad offers to piece together the surviving fragments of Gnostic teaching, which the established religions had tried to destroy:

> the bitter central truth of the gnostics: the horrifying realisation that the world of the Good God was a dead one, and that He had been replaced by a usurper – a God of Evil . . . It was the deep realisation of this truth, and its proclamation that had caused the gnostics to be suppressed, censored, destroyed. Humanity is too frail to face the truth about things – but to anyone who confronts the reality of nature and of process with a clear mind, the answer is completely inescapable: Evil rules the day.

What sort of God, the gnostic asks himself, could have organised things the way they are – this munching world of death and dissolution which pretends to have a Saviour, and a fountain of good at its base? What sort of God could have built this malefic machine of destruction, of self-immolation? Only the very spirit of the dark negative death-trend in nature – the spirit of nothingness and auto-annihilation. A world in which we are each other's food, each other's prey . . .

Seeing the world as an evil piece of work, the Gnostics advanced a new vision of freedom. Humans were no longer part of a scheme of things in which freedom meant obedience to law. To be free, humans must revolt against the laws that govern earthly things. Refusing the constraints that go with being a fleshly creature, they must exit from the material world.

While modern science might seem inhospitable to this Gnostic vision, the opposite has proved to be the case. As we understand it today, the cosmos is no longer ruled by laws that express any overarching purpose – benign or otherwise. In fact the world we live in may not be a cosmos at all. The seeming laws of nature may be regularities that express no abiding laws, and for all we know the universe may be at bottom chaotic. Yet the project of liberating the spirit from the material world has not disappeared. The dream of finding freedom by rebelling against cosmic law has reappeared as the belief that humans can somehow make themselves masters of nature.

The crystallographer J. D. Bernal (1901–71) illustrates how Gnostic ideas infuse modern science. At one time ranked among Britain's most influential scientists, a lifelong communist and proud recipient of a Stalin Peace Prize, Bernal was convinced that a scientifically planned society was being created in the Soviet Union. But his ambitions went beyond the rational reconstruction of human institutions. He was convinced that science could effect a shift in evolution in which human beings would cease to be biological organisms. As the historian of science Philip Ball has described it, Bernal's dream was that human society would be replaced by 'a Utopia of post-human cyborgs with machine bodies created by surgical techniques'. Even this fantasy did not exhaust Bernal's ambitions. Further in the future, he envisioned 'an erasure of individuality and mortality' in which human beings would cease to be distinct physical entities.

In a passage in his book *The World, the Flesh and the Devil: An Enquiry into the Future of the Three Enemies of the Rational Soul*, Bernal spells out what he has in mind: 'Consciousness itself might end or vanish in a humanity that has become completely etherealized, losing the close-knit organism, becoming masses of atoms in space communicating by radiation, and ultimately perhaps resolving itself entirely into light.'

Bernal published his book in 1929, but ideas very like his are being promoted at the present time. Similar conceptions inform the vision of the Singularity of the futurologist and director of engineering at Google Ray Kurzweil – an explosive increase in knowledge that will enable humans to emancipate themselves from the material world and cease to be biological organisms. The subtitle of Kurzweil's book *The Singularity is Near* is *When Humans Transcend Biology*, and while the technologies involved are different – uploading brain information into cyberspace rather than using surgery to build a cyborg – the ultimate goal of freeing the human mind from confinement in matter is the same as Bernal's. The affinities between these ideas and Gnosticism are clear. Here as elsewhere, secular thinking is shaped by forgotten or repressed religion.

Whether ancient or modern, Gnosticism turns on two articles of faith. First there is the conviction that humans are sparks of consciousness confined in the material world. The Gnostics did not deny that order existed in the world; but they viewed this order as a manifestation of evil to which they refused to submit. For them the creator was at best a blunderer, negligent or forgetful of the world it had fashioned, and possibly senile, mad or long dead; it was a minor, insubordinate and malevolent demiurge that ruled the world. Trapped in a dark cosmos, human beings were kept in submission by a trance-like ignorance of their true situation. Here we come to the second formative idea: humans can escape this slavery by acquiring a special kind of knowledge. *Gnosis* is the Greek word for knowledge, and for Gnostics knowledge is the key to freedom.

As Gnostics see them, humans are ill-designed and badly made creatures, gifted or cursed with flickering insight into their actual condition. Once they eat of the Tree of Knowledge, they discover they are strangers in the universe. From that point onwards, they live at war with themselves and the world.

In asserting that the world is evil, the Gnostics parted company with more ancient ways of thinking. Ancient Egyptian and Indian religion saw the world as containing light and dark, good and bad, but these were a pair that alternated in cycles rather than being locked in any sort of cosmic struggle. Animist conceptions in which the world is an interplay of creative and destructive forces frame a similar view of things. In a universe of this kind the problem of evil that has tormented generations of apologists for monotheism does not exist.

The idea of evil as an active force may have originated with Zoroaster. An Iranian prophet who lived some centuries before Christ (the exact dates are disputed), Zoroaster not only viewed the world as the site of a war between light and dark but believed light could win. Some centuries later another Iranian prophet – Mani, the founder of Manichaeism – also affirmed that good could prevail, though he seems to have believed that victory was not assured. It may have been around this time that the sensation of wavering between alternatives crystallized into an idea of free will.

The idea of a demonic presence in the world emerged with dualistic faiths. It does not appear in the Hebrew Bible, where Satan features as an adversarial figure rather than a personification of evil. It is only in the New Testament that evil appears as a diabolical agency, and throughout its history Christianity has struggled to reconcile this notion of evil with belief in a God that is all good and all powerful.

A convert from the religion of Mani, Augustine tried to resolve the conundrum by suggesting that evil was the absence of goodness – a fall from grace that came about through the misuse of free will. But there always remained a strand in Christianity that saw good and evil as opposed forces. Composed in the early thirteenth century, the most systematic surviving work of Cathar theology, *The Book of the Two Principles*, asserts that along with the principle of good there is another principle, 'one of evil, who is mighty in iniquity, from whom the power of Satan and of darkness and all other powers which are inimical to the true Lord God are exclusively and essentially derived'. In support of this view, the Cathar tract goes on to quote Jesus saying (Matthew 7: 18), 'A good tree cannot being forth evil fruit, neither can a corrupt tree bring forth good fruit.'

However such sayings are interpreted, the Christian religion has always been compounded from conflicting elements. There is no pristine tradition at the back of Christianity, Gnosticism or any other religion. The search for origins ends with the discovery of fragments.

The idea of evil as it appears in modern secular thought is an inheritance from Christianity. To be sure, rationalists have repudiated the idea; but it is not long before they find they cannot do without it. What has been understood as evil in the past, they insist, is error – a product of ignorance that human beings can overcome. Here they are repeating a Zoroastrian theme, which was absorbed into later versions of monotheism: the belief that 'as the "lord of creation" man is at the forefront of the contest between the powers of Truth and Untruth.' But how to account for the fact that humankind is deaf to the voice of reason? At this point rationalists invoke sinister interests – wicked priests, profiteers from superstition, malignant enemies of enlightenment, secular incarnations of the forces of evil.

As so often is the case, secular thinking follows a pattern dictated by religion while suppressing religion's most valuable insights. Modern rationalists reject the idea of evil while being obsessed by it. Seeing themselves as embattled warriors in a struggle against darkness, it has not occurred to them to ask why humankind is so fond of the dark. They are left with the same problem of evil that faces religion. The difference is that religious believers know they face an insoluble difficulty, while secular believers do not.

Aware of the evil in themselves, traditional believers know it cannot be expelled from the world by human action. Lacking this saving insight, secular believers dream of creating a higher species. They have not noticed the fatal flaw in their schemes: any such species will be created by actually existing human beings.

DEMIURGY AND TAILORS' DUMMIES

With its Gnostic interpretation of the Genesis story, Kleist's essay fascinated generations of writers and poets. One of the most gifted to have taken up Kleist's story, and by far the most original, was Bruno Schulz, the Polish-Jewish writer and artist. In 'Treatise on Tailors' Dummies', subtitled by Schulz 'The Second

Book of Genesis', the narrator tells of 'a series of most interesting and most unusual lectures' given by his father, a 'metaphysical conjuror'. According to these speculative disquisitions, offered to an audience of young women at an evening sewing session, everything that lived was the work of a demiurge. But the demiurge in question was matter itself, which was neither lifeless nor set in fixed forms:

> 'The Demiurge,' said my father, 'has had no monopoly of creation, for creation is the privilege of all spirits. Matter has been given infinite fertility, inexhaustible vitality, and, at the same time, a seductive power of temptation which invites us to create as well . . . The whole of matter pulsates with infinite possibilities that send dull shivers through it. Waiting for the life-giving breath of the spirit, it is endlessly in motion. It entices us with a thousand sweet, soft, round shapes, which it blindly dreams up within itself.'

In Schulz's version, the demiurge – blind, senseless, creative matter – gives birth to beings imbued with a similar impulse of creation. Once they are conscious, these creatures want to be the demiurge themselves:

> 'We have lived for too long under the terror of the matchless perfection of the Demiurge,' my father

said. 'For too long the perfection of his creation has paralyzed our own creative instinct. We don't wish to compete with him. We have no ambition to emulate him. We wish to be creators in our own, lower sphere; we want to have the privilege of creation, we want creative delights, we want – in one word – Demiurgy.'

In Schulz's retelling, humans act the part of a demiurge in a material world in which they find themselves by chance. The accidental product of an impersonal process, they cannot claim to be the purpose of creation. Yet a tendency to some kind of conscious awareness might almost seem to be innate in matter's workings, and humans appear bent on developing this tendency to the utmost degree. Human beings are like the tailors' dummies in his fabric shop, the narrator's father suggests:

> Figures in a waxwork museum . . . even fairground parodies of dummies, must not be treated lightly. Matter never makes jokes; it is always full of the tragically serious. Who dares to think you can play with matter, that you can shape it for a joke, that the joke will not be built in, will not eat into it like fate, like destiny? Can you imagine the pain, the dull imprisoned suffering, hewn into the matter of that dummy which does not know why it must be

what it is, why it must remain in that forcibly imposed form which is no more than a parody?

Humans have long been possessed by the dream of creating superior versions of themselves: the homunculi and golems of medieval legends; in modern times, thinking machines that are far better calculators than humans could ever be and potentially also more self-aware:

> 'The Demiurge was in love with consummate, superb, and complicated materials; we shall give priority to trash. We are simply entranced and enchanted by the cheapness, shabbiness and inferiority of material ... In one word,' Father concluded, 'we wish to create man a second time – in the shape and semblance of a tailors' dummy.'

With 'esoteric solemnity', the narrator's father – 'the inspired Heresiarch' – expounds his version of the Gnostic myth. The Demiurge:

> was in possession of important and interesting creative recipes. Thanks to them, he created a multiplicity of species which renew themselves by their own devices. No one knows whether these recipes will ever be reconstructed. But this is unnecessary, because even if the classical methods of creation

should prove inaccessible for evermore, there still remain some illegal methods, an infinity of heretical and criminal methods.

Translated from the language of Gnostic religion, this is a vision that animates much of modern science.

In Schulz's incomparably subtle tale, the narrator's father articulates the vision implicit in much of modern science: humankind may be a sport of nature, but having chanced into the world the human animal can use its growing knowledge to recreate itself in a higher form. Embodied in a cult of evolution, it is an unwitting version of demiurgy.

At once lyrical and ironic, Schulz's treatise reflects the character of its author. Schulz produced a large body of work in which magic is revealed in the most mundane things: the interior of a shop can be an entire world, its cheap and shoddy goods forming a sublime landscape; the story of a family can have the qualities of an ancient saga. It was through myth, Schulz believed, that human life was best understood. In an essay, 'The Mythicization of Reality', written in 1936, he wrote: 'Not one scrap of an idea of ours does not originate in myth, isn't transformed, mutilated, denatured mythology.'

In the myth that inspires Schulz's writings, individuality is a type of theatrical display, in which matter assumes a temporary role – a human, a cockroach – and moves on. Demiurgy is a continuation of this process. When humans pursue the dream of creating higher versions of themselves they obey matter's imperative, and their creations will be different from anything they can imagine.

Born in 1892 into a merchant family in the small town of Drohobych in the Galician province of the Austro-Hungarian Empire, Schulz spent his life at the epicentre of twentieth-century European barbarism. Attracted to art but unable to make a living from it and inheriting a family obligation to support ailing relatives, he became a teacher in a local school. Taking time and energy from his creative work, he found the job frustrating. An engagement to a woman to whom he was deeply attached, a Jewish convert to Catholicism, fell through. But though his outward life may have been unsatisfying, Schulz continued to produce work – stories, paintings, drawings – of radiant power.

Now in Ukraine, his birthplace was occupied during the Second World War by both Soviet and Nazi forces. During the Nazi period Schulz lived in the ghetto, but was for a time employed by a Nazi officer, who in return for painting murals on the walls of the playroom of his child gave Schulz food rations and a degree of protection. Aware of the deportations and executions of Jews that were under way, Schulz deposited parcels of his work with non-Jewish friends. On 19 November 1942, not long after finishing the murals, Schulz was shot dead by another Nazi officer while walking back to the ghetto carrying a loaf of bread. Schulz's protector had killed a Jew who was under the other officer's control, and the officer felt entitled to murder Schulz in return. 'You killed my Jew,' he was reported as boasting, 'so I killed yours.'

There is evidence that at the time he was murdered Schulz was preparing his escape, collecting money and false papers from friends in Warsaw. He may have been planning to flee Drohobych that very night (though where he would have fled is unclear). Much of Schulz's work has vanished without trace. The murals were discovered, some sixty years later, in what had become the pantry of the house where the Nazi officer had lived. Schulz's luminous spirit lives on in stories such as 'Tailors' Dummies', a playfully mocking rendition of a pervasive modern myth.

LEOPARDI AND THE SOULS OF MACHINES

In Kleist's essay humans are caught between the graceful automatism of the puppet and the conscious freedom of a god. The jerky, stuttering quality of their actions comes from their feeling that they must determine the course of their lives. Other animals live without having to choose their path through life. Whatever uncertainty they may feel sniffing their way through the world is not a permanent condition; once they reach a place of safety, they are at rest. In contrast, human life is spent anxiously deciding how to live.

Not long after Kleist wrote his essay, another view of what it means for humans to be free was presented by the Italian poet Giacomo Leopardi. Remembered as the author of exquisitely melancholy verse, Leopardi has been seen as belonging in the Romantic Movement. But his view of humans and their place in nature is in practice at the opposite extreme from that of the Romantics. Romantic thinking tends towards a cult of the infinite, whereas for Leopardi finitude and constraint are necessary for anything that can be described as civilized life. The sickness of the age, he believed, came from intoxication with the power given by science together with an inability to accept the mechanical world that science has revealed. If there was a cure for this malady, it required the conscious cultivation of illusions.

Apart from his verse, only a few short essays and dialogues of Leopardi's were published during his lifetime. A full version of his diagnosis of the modern malady did not appear in Italian until 1898, the centenary of his birth, while a complete translation into English was published only in 2013. Composed in secret and comprising some 4,500 handwritten pages, Leopardi's *Zibaldone* – a 'hodgepodge of thoughts' – was meant as a series of memos to himself. Ranging across ancient history and philology, the critique of religion and a new version of materialism, the *Zibaldone* is a methodical dissection of the belief that scientific knowledge can be the instrument of human liberation.

Much of the *Zibaldone* was written when Leopardi was in his early twenties in the library of his family home in the hill town of Recanati, a backwater in the Papal States, where his old-fashioned father still wore the sword showing he belonged to a princely caste. Developing poor sight and a hunchback from the long days he spent crouched in the library, where he taught himself Greek and Hebrew, Leopardi was frail and sickly most of his life. Forming few human attachments apart from an unsuccessful involvement with a married Florentine woman and suffering several long spells of poverty, he spent his last years living in Naples with a close male friend.

The delicate poet was also a merciless critic of modern ideals. He could not take seriously the modern idea that the human animal is improving. Some civilizations are better than others, he accepted, but none of them marks out a path for humankind. 'Modern civilization must not be considered simply as a continuation of ancient civilization, as its progression . . . these two civilizations, which are essentially different, are and must be considered as two separate civilizations, or rather two different and distinct species of civilization, each actually complete in itself.' Between these two Leopardi's sympathies were with the ancient world, whose way of life he believed was more conducive to happiness. Yet he never imagined that that world could be revived.

In Leopardi's account, modern civilization is driven by the increase of knowledge. Knowing more than any previous generation, humanity has cast off the illusions of the past – including religion. But this refusal of religion is itself partly a by-product of Christianity, and the result is to spawn illusions that are even more harmful.

The polytheistic cults of ancient times might be no more than products of the human imagination; but they helped humans live in a world of which they were ignorant and did not pretend to contain any universal truth. With its claim to be a revelation for all the world, Christianity undermined this tolerant acceptance of illusion. But the ancient world already contained the germ of its dissolution in philosophy. The habit of sceptical inquiry had produced a paralysing condition of uncertainty, which Christianity offered to heal. Christians believe their faith showed the ancient world the truth, and saved it from doubt.

For Leopardi, this was back to front:

> What was destroying the [ancient] world was the lack of illusions. Christianity saved it, not because it was the truth but because it was a new source of illusions. And the effects it produced, enthusiasm, fanaticism, magnanimous sacrifice, and heroism, are the usual effects of any great illusion. We are considering here not whether it is true or false but only that this proves nothing in its favour. But how did it establish itself amid so many obstacles . . . ? No one understands the human heart at all who does not recognize how vast is its capacity for illusions, even when these are contrary to its interests, or how often it loves the very thing that is obviously harmful to it.

The advance of reason has the effect of weakening illusions that are necessary to civilization:

> there is no doubt that the progress of reason and the extinction of illusions produce barbarism . . . The greatest enemy of barbarism is not reason but nature. Nature (if properly followed, however) provides us with illusions that, in their right place, make a people truly civilized . . . Illusions

> are natural, inherent to the system of the world. When they are removed completely or almost completely, man is denatured, and every denatured people is barbarous . . . And reason, by making us naturally inclined to pursue our own advantage, and removing the illusions that bind us to one another, dissolves society absolutely and turns people to savagery.

According to Leopardi the rise of Christianity was a response to an excess of doubt. Many of the ancient philosophers were inspired by visions of an invisible order of things. Pythagoras, Plato and their disciples believed a hidden harmony lay beyond or beneath the flux of human events. But the systematic doubt these philosophers practised proved more powerful than their mystical visions, and the result was a state of inner chaos that required a new and more potent illusion. In modern times this interplay has recurred in another form. Just as Christianity was a response to scepticism, secular faiths are a reaction against the decay of Christianity. Struggling to escape from the world that science has revealed, humanity has taken refuge in the illusion that science enables them to remake the world in their own image.

A feature of Leopardi's view of the world is his uncompromising materialism. Everything that exists is a type of matter, he believed, including what we call the soul. We are reluctant to give up the distinction between matter and mind because we cannot imagine matter thinking. But, for Leopardi, the fact that we think shows that matter thinks:

> That matter thinks is a fact. It is a fact because we ourselves think; and we do not know, we are not aware of being, we are not capable of knowing, of perceiving anything but matter. It is a fact because we see that the modifications of thought depend entirely on sensations, upon our physical state, and that our mind fully corresponds to the changes and variations in our body. It is a fact, because we feel our thought corporeally.

It is usually thought that a materialist such as Leopardi must reject religion, but this was not his view. Certainly religion was an illusion, but he knew that humans cannot live without illusions. He criticized Christianity, but his objections were not so much intellectual as moral and aesthetic: he attacked the Christian religion because of its impact on the quality of life.

Devaluing the natural world for the sake of a spiritual realm, Christianity could not be other than hostile to happiness: 'man', Leopardi wrote, 'was happier before Christianity than after it.' He was not what people today call a moral relativist – someone who thinks human values are just cultural constructions. He insisted on the constancy of human nature and its corollary, the existence of goods and evils that are universally human. What he rejected was turning these often conflicting values into a system of universal principles. Whether in Christianity or its secular successors any such project is bound to result in tyranny, since it is an attempt to suppress the irresolvable contradictions of human needs.

In Leopardi's view, the universal claims of Christianity were a licence for universal savagery. Because it is directed to all of humanity, the Christian religion is usually praised, even by its critics, as an advance on Judaism. Leopardi – like Freud a hundred years later – did not share this view. The crimes of medieval Christendom were worse than those of antiquity, he believed, precisely because they could be defended as applying universal principles: the villainy introduced into the world by Christianity was 'entirely new and more terrible . . . more horrible and more barbarous than that of antiquity'.

Modern rationalism renews the central error of Christianity – the claim to have revealed the good life for all of humankind. Leopardi described the secular creeds that emerged in modern times as expressions of 'half-philosophy', a type of thinking with many of the defects of religion. What Leopardi called 'the barbarism of reason' – the project of remaking the world on a more rational model – was the militant evangelism of Christianity in a more dangerous form.

Events have confirmed Leopardi's diagnosis. As Christianity has waned, the intolerance it bequeathed to the world has only grown more destructive. From imperialism through communism and incessant wars launched to promote democracy and human rights, the most barbarous forms of violence have been promoted as means to a higher civilization.

For all his attacks on Christianity, Leopardi did not welcome its decline. 'Religion', he wrote, 'is all we have to shore up the wretched and tottering edifice of present-day human life.' Yet there is no reason to think he derived any consolation from the faith he had inherited. Brought up by his father to be a good Catholic, he became an atheist who admired polytheism. Realizing that the more benign faiths of ancient times could not be revived, he defended the religion of his own time as the least harmful illusion. But he was incapable of surrendering to that illusion himself. Instead, he made a life from disillusion.

For Leopardi the human animal was a thinking machine. This is the true lesson of materialism, and he embraced it. Humans are part of the flux of matter. Aware that they are trapped in the material world, they cannot escape from this confinement except in death. The good life begins when they accept this fact. As he wrote in one of his most celebrated poems:

> . . . I recall the eternal,
> And the dead seasons, and the present one
> Alive, and all the sound of it. And so
> In this immensity my thought is drowned:
> And I enjoy my sinking in this sea.

Here Leopardi is at the furthest remove from the Gnostics, and yet his conception of the universe has something important in common with theirs.

Mind was not for Leopardi (as it was for the Gnostics) injected into matter from somewhere beyond the physical world. Matter was itself intelligent, constantly mutating and producing new forms, some of them self-aware. As a child Leopardi had written an essay on 'the souls of beasts', and he is clear that consciousness is not confined to humans. The difference between beasts and human beings is not that humans are self-aware while beasts are not. Both are conscious machines. The difference lies in the greater frailty of the human soul, which produces illusions of which beasts have no need.

In his superb 'Dialogue between Nature and an Icelander', published in 1824, Leopardi has Nature responding to the question whether it made the world 'expressly to torment us'. Nature asks the Icelander:

> Did you really think that the world was made for your sake? You need to understand that in my

works, in my ordinances, and in my operations, with very few exceptions, I always had and still have in mind something quite other than the happiness or unhappiness of men. When I hurt you in any way or by any means, I am not aware of it, except very seldom; just as, usually, if I please you or benefit you, I do not know of it; and I have not, as you believe, made certain things, nor do I perform certain actions, to please you or to help you. And finally, even if I happened to exterminate your whole race, I would not be aware of it . . .

. . . Obviously you have given no thought to the fact that the life of this universe is a perpetual cycle of production and destruction, the two connected in such a way that each continually serves the other, to ensure the conservation of the world, which as soon as one or the other of them ceased to be would likewise disintegrate. So the world itself would be harmed if anything in it were free from suffering.

For Leopardi evil is integral to the way the world works; but when he talks of evil he does not mean any kind of malign agency of the sort that Gnostics imagined. Evil is the suffering that is built into the scheme of things. 'What hope is there when evil is *ordinary*?' he asks. 'I mean, in an order where evil is *necessary*?' These rhetorical questions show why Leopardi had no interest in projects of revolution and reform. No type of human action – least of all the harlequinade of politics – could fundamentally alter a world in which evil was ordinary. It is not that Leopardi lacked human sympathy. Rather, he affirmed the irresponsibility and innocence of humankind. Understanding the necessity of evil, he thought, leads to compassion: 'My philosophy not only does not lead to misanthropy, as might seem to anyone who looks at it superficially, and as many accuse it of doing . . . My philosophy makes nature guilty of everything, and by exonerating humanity altogether, it redirects the hatred, or at least the complaint, to a higher principle, the true origin of the ills of living beings.' Human vices – greed, cruelty, deception – are natural. Nature is neither malign nor benevolent, but simply indifferent. Humans are machines that through a succession of random chances have become self-aware. Inner freedom – the only kind of freedom possible, he believed – is achieved by accepting this situation.

Leopardi did accept it. He would not have been surprised that much of his work was for so long unknown. Realizing that the human mind may decay as human knowledge advances, he did not expect his way of thinking to be appreciated or understood. Nor did he try to escape the end that comes to everything that lives. Immortality, he wrote in one of his most lovely verses, 'The Setting of the Moon', would be 'the worst of all our ills'. Calmly dictating the poem's closing lines as he lay dying in Naples, he seems to have seen his short life as complete in itself.

THE RETURN OF LIGEIA

With its faith that humankind can emancipate itself from natural limits by using the power of increasing knowledge, Gnostic thinking informs much of modern science. But a similar refusal of limitation can be found in currents of thought that are hostile to science. The Romantic Movement also asserted that humankind can remake the world – though not by using the power of reason. It was human will that would enable humankind to prevail over its natural condition. If the will was strong enough, even death could be conquered.

One version of this Romantic tradition is expressed in Edgar Allan Poe's 'Ligeia' (1838). The epigraph to the tale is a quote attributed to the seventeenth-century writer Joseph Glanvill: 'And the will therein lieth, which dieth not. Who knoweth the mysteries of the will, with its vigour? For God is but a great will pervading all things by nature of its intentness. Man doth not yield himself to the angels, nor unto death utterly, save only through the weakness of his feeble will.' The passage Poe cites has never been found, and it may be one he invented. If so it was an astute intuition that led him to attribute his invention to Glanvill.

A thoroughgoing sceptic as well as a pious clergyman, Glanvill (1636–80) used a method of doubt to demolish the hierarchical cosmos that medieval thinkers had built from ideas inherited from Greek philosophy. In one of his main works, *Scepsis Scientifica, or Confest Ignorance: The Way to Science* (first published as *The Vanity of Dogmatizing* in 1661), he argued that human beings can never have knowledge of cause and effect. All we have are impressions and beliefs, which give us the sense that the world follows an orderly course. We puff up these sensations into a system of rational principles that tells us that some things are necessary and others impossible. In truth we cannot know: 'We may affirm, that things are thus and thus, according to the Principles we have espoused: But we strangely forget ourselves, when we plead a necessity of their being so in Nature, and an Impossibility of their being otherwise.' Like the eighteenth-century Scottish sceptic David Hume, Glanvill denied that the human mind can know the causes of the events it observes. Unlike Hume, who used his sceptical philosophy to attack religion, Glanvill used doubt to defend faith – not only in the existence of God but also in witchcraft. In each case he asserted that faith was based in human experience.

Glanvill's sceptical doubt was one of the earliest expressions of modern empiricism and one of the most radical. As an epigraph to another of his stories, 'A Descent into the Maelström' (1841), Poe used a genuine quote from Glanvill, slightly altered, which reads: 'The ways of God in Nature, as in Providence, are not as our ways; nor are the models that we frame any way commensurate to the vastness, profundity, and unsearchableness of His works, which have a depth in them greater than the well of Democritus.' Poe was an admirer of Democritus, who believed that we live in a boundless universe made of atoms and the void. For the ancient Greek materialist philosopher, truth lies at the bottom of a well, the water of which serves as a mirror in which objects are reflected. But the addition of one word to the quote – 'unsearchableness' – suggests a closer affinity with Glanvill. For Poe, human reason could never grasp the nature of things. The world that we know is a work of the imagination – and none the worse for that, since what is fashioned by the human mind may have a greater perfection (Poe believed) than anything in the natural world.

Poe explored this thought in 'The Domain of Arnheim' (1842). Telling of a young man of great wealth who aimed to create a landscape 'whose combined vastness and definitiveness – whose united beauty, magnificence and *strangeness*, shall convey the idea of care, or culture, or superintendence, on the part of beings superior, yet akin to humanity', the story shows the gardener in the position of 'an intermediary or secondary nature – a nature which is not God, nor an emanation from God, but which is still nature in the sense of the handiwork of the angels that hover between man and God'. The artist-gardener is a demiurge crafting a scene more beautiful than any in the natural world.

In 'Ligeia', human artifice has an even greater role. The unnamed narrator describes a series of events in which he marries a woman of beauty, knowledge and intellect, who guides him into regions of 'metaphysical investigation'. Ligeia dies, the narrator remarries, only for his new spouse Rowena to die as well. But he keeps watch over her body, and during the vigil sees life returning and a familiar face – not that of Rowena, but instead that of Ligeia. As the quote from Glanvill hinted, death was annulled by human will.

Poe's life reveals no such will. It may be that – as a sympathetic biographer has it – he was 'fated to die in ignominy . . . darkness was always rushing towards him.' Born in 1809 and orphaned a year later, unable to find any steady source of income or settle into a career, founding magazines that failed and remaining extremely poor for most of his life, suffering many kinds of mania and obsession and seeking relief from them in drink, this inordinate genius was found wandering the streets of Baltimore, wearing someone else's clothes, incapable of coherent speech and unable to explain how he had come to this desperate pass. He was taken to a hospital, where he died on 7 October 1849.

'Ligeia' illustrates a Gnostic vision of a highly unusual kind. The narrator's reference to 'metaphysical investigation' may point back to alchemy, but might just as well refer to the practice of mesmerism that was so popular when Poe wrote. For Poe as for Glanvill, however, it was not modern science or hermetic wisdom that opened up the possibility of the will triumphing over the flesh but the most radical kind of doubt.

THE GOLEM AND THE CIRCULAR RUINS

The idea that humans might fashion a higher species surfaced repeatedly throughout the nineteenth century. Mary Shelley's *Frankenstein: or, The Modern Prometheus* (1818) explores what it would be for a human being to act as a demiurge. Publishing the book while Leopardi was writing the *Zibaldone*, Shelley recognized that any such homunculus could only be a monstrous embodiment of human pride.

(The two writers coincided in Italy for a time and had common acquaintances but did not meet, and it seems neither read the other.) Later in the nineteenth century, the Symbolist Villiers de L'Isle-Adam produced *Tomorrow's Eve* (1886), a novelistic account of the creation of a female 'android' – a term the writer coined. When humans take the place of the demiurge in these tales, things always end badly. Creating an artificial human being was an attempt to defy natural law – a modern version of the alchemist's dream.

Using ideas borrowed loosely from Kabbalah, the Austrian occultist writer Gustav Meyrink's *The Golem* (1915) is another fiction in this genre. According to J. L. Borges, Meyrink's book was 'the story of a dream; within this dream there are dreams, and within those dreams (I believe) other dreams.'

Fashioning a higher humanity is a dream whose absurdity goes unnoticed until reality, or another dream, dissipates the imaginary being. Even when they are explicitly designed to eliminate human flaws, artificial humans cannot escape the limitations of their creators. Fastening on features of the human animal they deem to be good, modern secular thinkers believe humankind can be recreated in a higher form that possesses only those features. It does not occur to these sublime moralists that in human beings the good and the bad may be intermixed. Knowing little of the world or themselves, they are unaware that the human good is not a harmonious whole; gracious and lovely ways of life may be the offspring of tyranny and oppression, while delicate virtues may rely for their existence on the most sordid human traits. Eradicating evil may produce a new species, but not the one its innocent creators had in mind. Humans have too little self-knowledge to be able to fashion a higher version of themselves.

Borges pursued the idea that a new humanity might be dreamt into being in one of his richest fictions, 'The Circular Ruins'. The story describes a travelling magician who finds a place to sleep in a burial niche in the ruins of the sanctuary of the fire god. 'The purpose which guided him was not impossible, though it was supernatural. He wanted to dream a man: he wanted to dream him with minute integrity and insert him into reality.' The magician knows the difficulty of the task: 'He comprehended that the effort to mould the incoherent and vertiginous matter dreams are made of was the most arduous task a man could undertake, though he might penetrate all the enigmas of the upper and lower orders: much more arduous than weaving a rope of sand or coining the faceless wind.'

The magician succeeds in dreaming a man into being; but in the dream the man is asleep, and cannot act or exist by himself. The magician finds himself in the position of a failed demiurge: 'In the Gnostic cosmogonies, the demiurgi knead and mould a red Adam who cannot stand alone: as unskilful and crude and elementary as this Adam of dust was the Adam of dreams fabricated by the magician's nights of effort.' The magician dreams the man he has dreamt into wakefulness. In order to conceal from the man, whom the magician now thinks of as his son, the fact that he is only a dream, he instils into his creation an invincible ignorance of his origins. 'Not to be a man, to be the projection of another man's dream, what a feeling of humiliation, of vertigo!'

The magician dreams that only he and the fire god know that his son is no more than a dream. But then, in what seems like a conflagration that has happened many times before, the fire god's sanctuary is itself consumed by fire. First the magician thinks of escape; but, reflecting on his labours and his old age, he walks into the flames, which consume him without any pain. It is then that the magician understands that he too – like the man he had dreamt – 'was a mere appearance, dreamt by another'.

Less perceptive than the shaman, those who aim to fashion a higher humanity with the aid of science think they are bringing purpose into the drift of matter. In fact they are themselves driven by matter's aimless energy. As in Borges's story, the modern scientific shaman and a new human species are both of them dreams.

SOLARIS AND OUR WORLD

Seemingly conscious, certainly alive, the vast water-covered planet of Solaris is engaged in a continuous process of self-transformation. In the Polish writer Stanislav Lem's 1961 novel *Solaris*, what motivates this self-transformation remains in doubt. The book has been read as an exploration of the impossibility of understanding an alien mind. In another reading – which is not inconsistent with the first – Lem's novel may be a parable of the search for God. Some such interpretation is hinted in Andrei Tarkovsky's film *Solaris* (1972).

The psychologist Kris Kelvin, who arrives on a research station floating above the watery surface, is one of several generations of scientists who travel to Solaris in order to study the planet. Once they find they are dealing with a living intelligence, the scientists try to make contact with it. You might think they want to engage with a non-human mind, but one of the scientists doubts that this is the motive: 'We don't want to conquer the cosmos, we simply want to extend the boundaries of Earth to the frontiers of the cosmos ... We are only seeking Man. We have no need of other worlds.' In seeking to enter the mind of the planet, the scientists may be trying to understand themselves.

The sentience of the planet was not accepted from the start. (There were some who never accepted it.) Circling around two suns, one red and one blue, Solaris maintained an orbit that, according to the laws of gravitation, ought to be inherently unstable. This led to the discovery that the ocean was capable of exerting an active influence on the planet's orbital path, and what had been the established scientific world-view was threatened. It was attempts to probe further into the ocean using specially designed electronic instruments that led many scientists to conclude that the ocean was sentient.

The planet took an active part in the investigation by remodelling the instruments as they were operating. How it intervened in their experiments, and for what reason, could not be known. No two interventions were the same; sometimes there was total silence. But over time, it became possible to classify the planet's responses into what seemed to be intelligible patterns.

The vast inhuman mind was not only cogitating. It was constantly creating new forms, a teeming diversity of shapes and structures, a few of which the scientists were able to classify: 'tree-mountains', 'extensors', 'fungoids', 'mimoids', 'symmetriads' and 'asymmetriads', 'vertebrids' and 'agilus' . . . The ocean's creativity proved to be even more astonishing when it began fashioning a succession of visitors – simulacra of human beings – for the scientists who came to study it. Why it did so would never be known.

The visitors included Rheya, Kelvin's late wife, who had committed suicide after a quarrel with her husband. Fully conscious but with no memory of the past, or any understanding of how she came to be in the research station, Rheya is puzzled, and then distressed. So is Kelvin, who tries to rid himself of her by tricking her into a shuttle and firing it off into space. But Rheya – or another likeness of her – returns. More troubled than before, she kills herself.

Kelvin is left alone with the mystery of the ocean. He would like the Rheya he knew and loved on Earth to return, but accepts that this is impossible: 'We all know that we are material creatures, subject to the laws of physiology and physics, and not even the power of all our feelings combined can defeat those laws. All we can do is detest them.' He does not believe the ocean would respond to the tragedy of two human beings. Descending to the ocean's surface and landing on a soft, porous island that resembles the ruins of an ancient town after it has been devastated by an earthquake, Kelvin asks himself whether he must go on living on this inscrutable planet. 'I hoped for nothing. And yet I lived in expectation . . . I knew nothing, and

I persisted in the faith that the time of cruel miracles was not past.'

Solaris views the human world with a serene lack of concern. A part of the impulse to make contact with the ocean comes from the belief that it must have goals like those of humans. But while the ocean has capacities for self-awareness and intentional action – possibly greater than those of any human being – it lacks the needs these capacities serve in humans. If it finds pleasure in playing with the scientists, there is nothing to suggest that it welcomes their attentions. It shows no sympathy for the anguish of the human simulacra it creates. It wants nothing from humans. If they depart or disappear, it will feel no loss. The process of self-transformation will go on.

Tarkovsky's film ends with Kelvin finding himself walking through woods past a pond towards his father's wooden house. A dog runs towards him, which he greets warmly. Looking through the window of the house, he sees his father in a room through which rain is pouring. He walks around the house to a back door, where he meets and embraces his father. At that point the camera pulls back, and the viewer sees that the house and its surroundings are breaking up and vanishing into the ocean foam.

Like any true myth, Lem's *Solaris* has no single meaning. But one possible interpretation is that humans live already in a world like that of Solaris. Wherever they look, humans see forms and structures; but these shapes may be deceptive. The human world may be like the home Kelvin sees on the island – an insubstantial makeshift that is forever tumbling and falling away.

THE REVELATION OF PHILIP K. DICK

It would be hard to find a more striking statement of a Gnostic world-view than this:

> Behind the counterfeit universe lies God . . . It is not a man who is estranged from God; it is God who is estranged from God. He evidently willed it this way at the beginning, and has never since sought his way back home. Perhaps it can be said that he has inflicted ignorance, forgetfulness, and suffering – alienation and homelessness – on Himself . . . He no longer knows why he has done all this to himself. He does not remember.

Having undergone a succession of experiences in which he seemed to gain access to another order of things, Dick found himself feeling at once liberated and oppressed. He recognized that these seemingly paranormal experiences might be accounted for by personal factors, including heavy drug use over many years, and did not deny that they involved a departure from conventional norms of sanity. Yet he remained convinced that he had been granted a glimpse of another world from which, along with all other human beings, he had been immemorially exiled:

> Within a system that must generate an enormous amount of veiling, it would be vainglorious to expostulate on what actuality is, when my premise declares that were we to penetrate to it for any reason, this strange, veil-like dream would reinstate itself retroactively, in terms of our perceptions and in terms of our memories. The mutual dreaming would resume as before, because, I think, we are like the characters in my novel *Ubik*; we are in a state of half-life. We are neither dead nor alive, but preserved in cold storage, waiting to be thawed out.

A brilliantly original writer of science fiction who used the genre to question what it means to be human, Philip K. Dick never came to terms with the upheaval that he suffered in the months of February–March 1974. He struggled with the experience for the rest of his life.

If the circumstances of his life led him to the experience, they also ensured that it would remain painfully enigmatic. Born prematurely along with his twin sister Jane in December 1928, Dick suffered states of what seems like metaphysical horror from his early years. Jane died six weeks after she was born, an event that troubled him throughout his life. He was terrified when his father put on a gas mask to illustrate stories of his time in the war: 'His face would disappear. This was not my father any longer. This was not a human being at all.' In 1963, he had a vision that harked back to this early terror: 'I looked up in the sky and saw a face. I didn't really see it, but the face was there, and it was not a human face; it was a vast visage of perfect evil . . . It was immense; it filled a quarter of the sky. It had empty slots for eyes – it was metal and cruel and, worst of all, it was God.'

Episodes such as this appeared in his fiction – the metal face in the sky became Palmer Eldritch, for example. They also pulled Dick in the direction of Gnosticism. As his biographer comments, for Dick 'the Gnostic view that our world is an illusory reality created by an evil, lesser deity was utterly compelling. It could account for the suffering of humankind, as well as for startling phenomena such as a vision of "absolute evil" (the Gnostic god's true visage!) in the sky.' This Gnostic vision resonated deeply with some aspects of Dick's personality, while other parts of him were just as deeply repelled by it.

Dick was always prone to paranoid fears, not always without reason. In late 1953 he and his then girlfriend were visited by FBI agents, who showed them surveillance photographs and appear to have offered them expense-free places at the University of Mexico if they agreed to spy on their fellow students. Such approaches were not unusual at the time. Overshadowed by the Cold War and McCarthyism, early Fifties America was a time of suspicion. Many years later, Dick discovered through a Freedom of Information request that a letter he had written to Soviet scientists in 1958 had been intercepted by the CIA. Surveillance of this kind was routine in these years, but it is unlikely that American intelligence agencies had any special interest in Dick. He had no access to sensitive information, and the costs of monitoring him would have been prohibitive. Even so, for the rest of his life Dick believed he was under surveillance – if not by the FBI then by the KGB or (perhaps worst of all) the Internal Revenue Service.

In late 1971 his house was burgled and his files removed – a break-in he attributed to Watergate-type Federal agents or possibly religious fundamentalists, among others. Neither explanation was entirely fantastical – this was the time of Nixon, and Dick had been involved in the late Sixties with James A. Pike, the Episcopal Bishop of California, in seances in which the bishop had attempted to make contact with his son, who had committed suicide. At the same time, neither explanation was realistically plausible. (Some among Dick's friends suspected he may have staged the break-in himself, perhaps to foil an anticipated IRS tax audit.) Following his mental upheaval in early 1974 he believed that his personality was being taken over by US Army Intelligence. He called the local police to tell them 'I am a machine', and wrote to the FBI in an attempt to dispel any doubts as to his loyalties. Such episodes suggest full-blown paranoia.

In the aftermath of his mental upheaval, Dick medicated himself with drugs, alcohol and vitamin preparations, while consulting a number of therapists. Yet he could not shake off the sense of confinement imposed on him by the revelation he had experienced. Instead of ascending to a realm where he would be free from danger, he saw himself ever after as being surrounded by evil forces. Fantasies of conspiracy – political or cosmic – dominated Dick's view of the world up to his death, some weeks after he suffered a stroke, in March 1982.

Dick's propensity to paranoia was exacerbated by his style of life – not least his excessive use of amphetamines. But his was paranoia of a peculiar kind, one that articulated an entire world-view – a highly distinctive version of Gnosticism. With its vision of the world as being ruled by an evil demiurge Gnosticism is, in effect, the metaphysical version of paranoia. Paranoid delusion is often a reaction against insignificance – the sense, often well founded, of counting for nothing in the world. Dick's paranoia was of this kind. By seeking a sense of significance, he became familiar with the dark side of a world where nothing is without meaning.

Dick's achievement as a writer came from detaching science fiction from speculation about the future and linking it with perennial questions about what can truly be known. In many of his novels and short stories he explored the dizzying possibility that the universe is an infinitely layered dream, in which every experience of illumination proves to be one more false awakening. This was the theme of novels such as *The Man in the High Castle* (1962), a novel of alternate history in which Axis forces are imagined as having won the Second World War and the chief protagonist ends unsure which history actually occurred; *The Three Stigmata of Palmer Eldritch* (1965), where an evil entrepreneur markets an alien hallucinogen that destroys the ability to distinguish the real from the unreal; *Valis* (1981), in which it appears that the central character is being helped to uncover the truth of things by an alien space probe; and *The*

Transmigration of Timothy Archer (1982), a posthumously published volume, dealing with the struggle of a renegade bishop to make sense of recently discovered Gnostic texts.

These novels reflected and sometimes anticipated experiences in which the author was unable to say what was real and what not. Often the life and the work were images of one another: Timothy Archer is an avatar of Bishop James Pike, for example. It was not just reality and illusion that were intertwined. So were fact and fiction. Dick could not accept that his life was shaped by a succession of random events – the death of his twin sister, a routine visit by the FBI, a commonplace break-in. He looked for design in everything that happened to him – above all his mental breakdown. Fearing he could not make sense of his experience, he turned it into a book.

The book was *The Exegesis*, a massive manuscript of over eight thousand pages and around two million words, mostly handwritten and not meant for publication, in which he tried to comprehend what he had undergone. The editors of the published version, which appeared in 2011, describe it as:

> visionary and fractured, at once coming apart and striving heroically, in the only way a novelist can strive for such a thing, to keep himself together as a life nears its end in shambles,

haunted by a dead twin sister whose own life was a month long, and defined by bouts of psychosis, a diorama of drugs, five marriages, suicide attempts, and financial destitution, real or imagined stalking by the FBI and IRS, literary rejection at its most stupid (which is to say destructive), and a Linda Ronstadt obsession.

Invoking early Christian teachings and a number of esoteric traditions, especially Gnosticism, Dick struggled to persuade himself that what he had experienced was an authentic revelation. Having been unhinged from reality for large parts of his life, he wanted to believe he was now on the way to being truly sane.

Though it was marked out by his own traumas, Dick trod a path that has been followed by many before him. Like human beings in every age he wanted to believe that the events of his life formed part of a pattern. So he created a story in which his life was shaped by secret agencies, some of them from beyond the human world. But a world in which nothing happens by chance is an enclosed space that soon proves maddening. Dick found himself stuck in such a place – not the radiant, meaning-filled cosmos he was looking for, but a dark prison. Scrawled on the walls were messages, some of which would appear later in the pages of his books.

The Exegesis is rambling, fragmented and often wildly speculative. The synthesis of personal experience with hermetic tradition at which he laboured was never achieved. Yet he succeeded in bringing together Gnostic themes that, unnoticed or repressed, shape much of modern thinking.

Dick summarized what his experiences had led him to believe:

1 the empirical world is not quite real, but only seemingly real;
2 its creator cannot be appealed to for a rectification or redress of these evils and imperfections;
3 the world is moving towards some kind of end state or goal, the nature of which is obscure, but the evolutionary aspect of the change states suggests a good and purposeful end state that has been designed by a sentient and benign proto-entity

In this cosmogony the visible world is the work of 'a limited entity termed "the artifact"'. The 'artifact', or demiurge, may be ignorant, or else (Dick sometimes speculated) demented. But it is not malevolent, simply doing what it can to free humans from delusion. This is a view that has something in common with Kabbalah, as Dick acknowledges:

Probably everything in the universe serves a good end . . . The *Sepher Yezirah*, a Cabbalist text, *The Book of Creation*, which is almost two thousand years old, tells us: 'God has also set the one over against the other; the good against the evil, and the evil against the good; the good proceeds from the good, and the evil from the evil; *the good purifies the bad, and the bad the good* [Dick's italics]; the good is preserved for the good, and the evil for the bad ones.'

Underlying the two game players there is God, who is neither and both. The effect of the game is that both players become purified. Thus the ancient Hebrew monotheism, so superior to our own view.

An interplay between good and evil in which each is necessary to the other is at the heart of many mystical traditions. If he had stuck to this view, Dick might have exorcized the demons that possessed him. But he needed to know, beyond any possibility of doubt, that the scheme of things was good. In 1975 he wrote: 'This is not an evil world, as Mani supposed. There is a good world under the evil. The evil is somehow superimposed over it (Maya), and when stripped away, pristine glowing creation is visible.'

The idea that evil is a veil covering the good is an old one. But it leaves unresolved the questions, why and from where did the veil appear? If it originated in some divine mind, the world must have been made by a creator that is itself partly evil. This creator may be only a lesser god, one of many. But how did this ambiguous demi-god come into being, if the true God is all good? Why must humans spend their lives struggling against illusion?

These are questions Dick could not answer. In Gnosticism evil and ignorance are one and the same; when *gnosis* is attained, evil vanishes – at least for the adept. In this type of illumination there can be no uncertainty. Dick's experience was nothing like this. The illumination he experienced was the trigger for a process of psychological disintegration. There was no way the revelation he had received could be seen as the end of his search. This may be why he introduced the idea of evolution into the system of ideas he was struggling to put together. Invoking a process of evolutionary change that is alien to Gnostic thought, Dick believed a transformation was under way that spanned vast tracts of human history and cosmic time. Believing that the human mind becomes gradually more enlightened, he was applying a near-universal modern assumption. In many respects an antinomian figure, he was also a product of his age.

A belief in human advance through time is built into the modern world-view. For Plato, the Gnostics and the early Christians, there was no question of the shadow-world of time moving towards any better state. Either time would literally end – as Jesus, the apocalyptic Jewish prophet who came to be seen as the founder of Christianity, appears to have believed – or else time and eternity coexisted in perpetuity, as Plato and the Gnostics thought. Either way there was no expectation that any fundamental alteration in human affairs could occur in the course of history. Taken for granted in the ancient world, this view of things is nowadays close to being incomprehensible.

The modern world inherits the Christian view in which salvation is played out in history. In Christian myth human events follow a design known only to God; the history of humankind is an ongoing story of redemption. This is an idea that informs virtually all of western thought – not least when it is intensely hostile to religion. From Christianity onwards, human salvation would be understood (at least in the west) as involving movement through time. All modern philosophies in which history is seen as a process of human emancipation – whether through revolutionary change or incremental improvement – are garbled versions of this Christian narrative, itself a garbled version of the original message of Jesus.

Dick wavered between accepting that history is ruled by chance and believing it obeys a secret design.

In 1980 he considered writing a novel of an alternate world, 'The Acts of Paul', which would have explored the radical contingency of history. In 'The Acts of Paul', Christianity – the faith that more than any other affirms that history has meaning – would have been clearly just a spin-off from random events. Sadly, the novel was never written.

The belief that evolution is advancing towards some desirable end is ubiquitous, and Dick could not help being influenced by it. Above all, he was attracted to the idea of evolution because it promised that his epiphanies might someday make sense. If the mind evolved through time, his confusion need not be permanent. Dick wrote: 'What happened . . . is that I woke up to reality. But it has these counterfeit accretional layers over it. Our sense of time – of the passage of time – is the result of our scanning the changes of appearance . . . I merely passed over from unconscious messenger to conscious . . .'

Some months before he died Dick wrote a letter enclosing a one-page 'final statement' of *The Exegesis*. Under the guidance of a 'hyper-structure', a new species with a higher level of awareness than humans was evolving. He insisted this was not 'mere faith'. But for him it had to be true. He could not live without the belief that his disorienting experiences were phases in a continuing process of enlightenment. Desperate for any kind of meaning, Dick needed a fantasy of evolution in order to avoid being left with mystery.

ENTERING THE ZONE

We like to think that if another intelligent species were to visit the Earth it would do so in order to interact with us – if not to communicate with us or study our behaviour, then at least to exploit or destroy us. In H. G. Wells's canonical tale of alien invasion *War of the Worlds* (1898), Martians invade the Earth because it is younger and warmer than their own planet; they aim to wipe out humanity in order to clear the way for themselves. In Michel Faber's subtle exploration of an alien view of humans, *Under the Skin* (2000), an extra-terrestrial assuming the form of an attractive young woman captures hitchhikers in order that their flesh can be prepared as meat and consumed as a delicacy by her fellow aliens. In each of these classics, humans have some value and significance for the alien visitants – even if that value is negative and their significance no more than instrumental. But what if alien visitors to the planet had no interest in humans at all?

A scenario of this kind is presented in Arkady and Boris Strugatsky's *Roadside Picnic*. First published in 1972 in a heavily censored and mutilated form as a series of stories in the former Soviet Union and turned by Andrei Tarkovsky into the film *Stalker* (1979), the novel tells of an alien Visitation to six places. Later labelled by scientists as 'Blind Quarters' and 'Plague Quarters', these are dangerous sites in which the laws of physics seem not to apply. They also contain artefacts that have become prized booty for 'stalkers' – illegal scavengers who risk their lives by entering the Zones in order to remove the objects and sell them on. How the artefacts work is unknown – as is the reason for the alien visitation.

But suppose the aliens had no special reason for visiting the Earth, and what they left behind was simply litter left over from a casual stop-over. One of the scientists studying the Zones speculates that this may in fact be the case:

> A picnic. Imagine: a forest, a country road, a meadow. A car pulls off the road into the meadow and unloads young men, bottles, picnic baskets, girls, transistor radios, cameras ... A fire is lit, tents are pitched, music is played. And in the morning they leave. The animals, birds and insects that were watching the whole night in horror crawl out of their shelters. And what do you see? An oil spill, a gasoline puddle, old spark plugs and oil filters strewn about ... Scattered rags, burnt-out bulbs, someone has dropped a monkey wrench. The

wheels have tracked mud from some godforsaken swamp . . . and, of course, there are the remains of the campfire, apple cores, candy wrappers, tins, bottles, someone's handkerchief, someone's penknife, old ragged newspapers, coins, wilted flowers from another meadow . . .

Among the alien artefacts are a black stick that produces unlimited energy with which to power machines, a 'death lamp' that destroys everything living around it, 'sprays' and 'needles' whose uses cannot be identified and a 'golden sphere' that grants all wishes. The 'stalkers' who risked death by entering the Zones in search of such items were not disturbed predators of the kind the word denotes in English. Boris Strugatsky tells us that when he and his brother were writing the book they took the Russian version of the word from a pre-revolutionary translation of Rudyard Kipling's *Stalky & Co.* (published in England in book form in 1899), a copy of which one of them picked up in a flea-market. When they used the word to describe the 'prospectors' who sought out valuables in the Zones, they meant to call up someone 'streetwise . . . a tough and even ruthless youth, who, however, was by no means without a certain boyish chivalry and generosity'.

When they ventured into the Zones, the stalkers were looking for something that would change their lives. The objects they found were unusable and often inexplicable. That did not diminish their worth. Quite the opposite: it was the fact that they could not be understood that made the objects so valuable. If they were intensely sought after, it was because they could not be grasped by the human mind.

For the majority, the alien visitation changes nothing. As the scientist puts it:

> We now know that for humanity as a whole, the Visit has largely passed without a trace. For humanity everything passes without a trace. Of course, it's possible that by randomly pulling chestnuts out of this fire, we'll eventually stumble on something that will make life on Earth completely unbearable . . . Humanity as a whole is too stable a system, nothing upsets it.

Even the stalkers hold back from what the aliens have left behind. In Tarkovsky's film, for which the Strugatsky brothers wrote the screenplay, the visitors have left a Room that has the power to realize anyone's most cherished dreams. Led through a wasteland by a stalker-guide, a writer and a professor reach the Room's antechamber. Along the way they talk of what they want when they enter the Room. The writer confesses that he covets a Nobel Prize, the professor says he has come to destroy the

Room because it is too dangerous for humankind, while the guide claims all he wants is to help those who are looking for the Room. The guide tells of another stalker, from whom he learnt everything he knows of the Room – a man called Porcupine, who used it to get rich and ended by hanging himself. When they reach the Room the professor decides it is no longer a threat and dismantles the explosive device he has brought with him. The three of them sit together in the antechamber, and after a while rain begins to seep through the ceiling. The film leaves open whether what the aliens have left behind has any human meaning at all. Perhaps the Room reveals what humans most want, and that is why it is so dangerous. Or perhaps the Room is empty. In any event, no one goes in.

MR WESTON DROPS A MATCH

'One would think almost that at the bottom of the well of being one may discover, instead of a mighty God, only the cap and bells of a mad fool.' The idea of a madcap God appears in *Unclay*, the story of how God's messenger John Death is sent to 'scythe' or 'unclay' two of the inhabitants of the small village of Dodder. Losing the parchment on which their names are written, Death decides to pass the summer in the village. A gay, wanton figure, he passes his time in sexual encounters with village women and rejoicing in his mission of bringing release to suffering humanity. 'Perhaps I am an illusion,' Death ruminates near the end of his stay. 'But, whether real or no, I am no enemy to man.'

Published in 1931, *Unclay* was the last novel of T. F. Powys and brings together many of the central themes of the reclusive Dorset writer's work. A profoundly religious man, Theodore Powys lived without the consolations of faith. 'I am without a belief,' he wrote. 'A belief is too easy a road to God.' When asked why he went so often to the church next to his cottage, it is said he replied, 'Because it's quiet.' When he was dying he declined to receive communion.

Born in 1875 the son of a clergyman and one of three brothers who became writers – the others were John Cowper Powys and Llewelyn Powys – Theodore married a local girl and lived most of his life in a series of remote villages. Refusing to travel and after some years as a farmer devoting himself to writing, he subsisted on a small inheritance from his father. His life was not always as reclusive as he may have wished. As his stories attracted the attention of some in the Bloomsbury Group, he received a stream of literary visitors. For a time he was almost famous. Today he is almost forgotten.

The village life that Powys chronicled was no rural

idyll. Like figures in a medieval woodcut, his villagers enact universal passions and endure the sorrows of human beings everywhere. In the human world as Powys saw it, nothing lasts; but neither does anything really change. It was a world he loved, and also wanted to leave behind.

Moved by these conflicting impulses, he turned orthodox religion upside down. Whether conceived as everlasting life in another world or an exit from time into eternity, immortality is the ardent hope of believers. Powys, on the other hand, cherished mortality. Far from death being the supreme evil, it lightens the burden of life. Nothing could be worse, he believed, than living for ever. Even God might come to yearn for the oblivion of death.

Powys's masterpiece *Mr Weston's Good Wine* (1927) tells how a wine merchant arrives in an old, mud-spattered Ford van on a dull November evening in the village of Folly Down. Accompanied by an assistant called Michael, Mr Weston is a short, stout man dressed in an overcoat and wearing a brown felt hat under which his hair is 'white like wool'. He has come to the village to sell his wines. The wine merchant 'had once written a prose poem that he had divided into many books', only to be surprised when he discovered 'the very persons and place that he had seen in fancy had a real existence in fact'.

Visiting the world he has unknowingly created, Mr

Weston wishes he could share the brief lives of human beings. He has come with two wines to sell – the light white wine of love and the dark wine of death. Asked if he drinks the dark wine himself, Mr Weston replies: 'The day will come when I hope to drink of it . . . but when I drink my own deadly wine the firm will end.' He longs for final death, the complete extinction from which the religion established in his name has promised to deliver humankind.

At the end of the story, having dispensed his wines in the village, he has Michael drive him to the summit of Folly Down hill, where the engine stops and the car's lights go out. He and Michael talk awhile, with Michael mentioning Mr Weston's 'old enemy'. Mr Weston asks, 'don't you think he would like to be a serpent again – a smaller adder?' Michael answers: 'I fancy . . . that he would prefer to disappear in his own element – fire.' Mr Weston is delighted.

> 'And so he shall!' cried Mr Weston. 'Will you be so kind, Michael, as to drop a burning match into the petrol tank?'
>
> 'And we?' asked Michael.
>
> 'Shall vanish in the smoke,' replied Mr Weston.
>
> 'Very well,' said Michael sadly.
>
> Michael did as he was told. In a moment a fierce tongue of flame leaped up from the car; a pillar of smoke rose above the flame and ascended into the

heavens. The fire died down, smouldered and went out.

Mr Weston was gone.

More subversive of established religion than any of the humanistic pieties of contemporary atheism, Powys's story portrays a God whose devoutest wish is to cease to exist. This self-annihilating God appears in a story Powys published in the same year as *Unclay*. *The Only Penitent* tells of the Reverend Hayhoe, a country vicar who asks his parishioners to come to him and confess their sins. Never doubting that they will welcome the opportunity to repent, he is puzzled when no one comes to confess and begins to doubt his faith. But then a solitary penitent turns up – a mad old man called Tinker Jar, of whom it was said that 'when the tinker wasn't walking upon the everlasting hills, he would use the storm clouds as a chariot.' Kneeling humbly before Mr Hayhoe, Tinker Jar tells him:

> 'I am the Only Penitent . . . I have come to confess my sin to you.'
>
> 'Can I give you absolution?' asked Mr Hayhoe, in a low tone.
>
> 'You can,' replied Jar, 'for only by the forgiveness of man can I be saved.'

Jar bowed his head and confessed his sins:

> 'I crucified my son . . . 'Twas I who created every terror in the earth, the rack, the plague, all despair, all torment . . . all pain and all evil are created by me.'

Mr Hayhoe responds by reminding Tinker Jar of the beauty of life – the love of a woman and the joy of those the tinker leads to dance in green pastures. The old man is unmoved.

> 'I destroy all men with a sword,' said Jar. 'I cast them down into the pit, they become nothing.'
>
> 'Hold!' cried Mr Hayhoe. 'Is that last word true?'
>
> 'It is,' answered Jar.
>
> 'Then, in the name of Man,' said Mr Hayhoe boldly, 'I forgive your sin; I pardon and deliver you from all your evil; confirm and strengthen you in all goodness, and bring you to everlasting death.'

If Theodore Powys believed in any God – which is doubtful – it was not that of Christianity. A demiurge baffled and saddened by its creation, Powys's God is filled with remorse at having created a world containing so much sorrow.

The picture Powys presents of the Jewish prophet

who came to be seen as the founder of Christianity is touched with Gnostic themes. A rebel against God who was disowned by humanity, Jesus came to destroy what Powys described in an early book, *Soliloquies of a Hermit* (1918), as 'our old happiness, our old Godhead, our old immortality'. Jesus tells us to forget any thought of immortality: by accepting our own extinction, we escape a world ruled by death. With this paradox at the heart of his work, Powys may seem like a Gnostic Christian. Yet he says nothing of any *gnosis*. It is the patient old Earth that endures and consoles. We may vanish from the scene, but the cycle of light and dark continues without end.

2 In the Puppet Theatre

I have seen
the winged man, and he was no
angel.

R. S. Thomas, 'The Refusal'

ROOF GARDENS, FEATHERS AND HUMAN SACRIFICE

'Our Lord, the lord of the near, of the nigh, is made to laugh. He is arbitrary, he is capricious, he mocketh . . . He is placing us in the palm of his hand; he is making us round. We roll; we become as pellets. He is casting us from side to side. We make him laugh; he is making a mockery of us.' This is how the last Aztec nobles, remnants of the civilization that was destroyed after the incursion into its territory of the Spanish conquistador Hernán Cortés in 1519, described their god – whose spirit they believed entered into their earthly ruler – in the Florentine Codex.

Named after the city where the original manuscript is kept, collected and transcribed thirty years after the conquest by a Franciscan missionary, the Codex presents a picture of a way of life that seems utterly alien to the modern mind. There are many today who, ascribing to the Aztecs needs and values they take to be universally human, cannot imagine a society in which these marks of humanity are absent. How could the Aztecs, fixed in rigid hierarchies, fail to want to choose the course of their lives? Surrounded as they were by ritual violence, how could they not feel revulsion? If the Codex does not reflect these impulses, it can only be because it portrays the Aztecs as less than human.

An alternative interpretation may be more interesting. If the Aztecs appear unrecognizably alien to the modern mind, it may be because the modern mind does not recognize itself in the Aztecs. We cannot understand the Aztecs because we do not want to understand ourselves.

Inga Clendinnen, a scholar with a profound insight into the Aztec way of life, writes:

> There is one activity for which the 'Aztecs' were notorious: the large-scale killing of humans in ritual sacrifices. The killings were not remote, top-of-the pyramid affairs. If only high priests and rulers killed, they carried out most of their butchers' work *en plein air*, and not only in the main temple precinct, but in the neighbourhood temples and on the streets. The people were implicated in the care

and preparation of the victims, their delivery to the place of death, and then in the elaborate processing of the bodies: the dismemberment and distribution of heads and limbs, flesh and blood and flayed skins. On high occasions warriors carrying gourds of human blood or wearing the dripping skins of their captives ran through the streets, to be ceremoniously welcomed into the dwellings; the flesh of their victims seethed in domestic cooking pots; human thighbones, scraped and dried, were set up in the courtyard of the households – and all this among a people notable for a precisely ordered polity, a grave formality of manner, and a developed regard for beauty.

The 'Aztecs' were several different peoples, each with characteristics they prized as proof of their distinctiveness. But life in the great lake city of Tenochtitlan, which was for two centuries the capital of the Aztec empire and had a population greater than any city in Spain at the time the conquerors arrived, expressed an understanding of what it means to be human that was shared by the larger family of 'Aztec' or Mexica communities. Giving central place to human impulses that modern thinking denies, it is a conception that shocks and horrifies today.

The feature of the Aztec capital that most impressed the conquerors was its order and cleanliness. Inured to the filth of European cities, some of the soldiers wondered if Tenochtitlan was a dream. Linked to the land by three causeways, the city was a vast settlement, with its aqueducts, dwellings and streets meticulously planned. Large or small, its houses were bright and elegant. 'All the buildings shone with whitewash and were bordered by ruler-straight canals and well-swept footpaths.' Green gardens had been cultivated on land reclaimed from the lake, while plants and flowers were grown on the roofs of the houses. The centre of a network of trade and tribute, the city was rich in precious metals. The walls of great courtyards were decorated, and the priests produced beautiful painted books. Topped with its Great Pyramid, the central temple precinct contained dozens of pools, temples and lesser pyramids.

Today a city of this kind would be seen as an embodiment of human reason. In fact, this majestic settlement was an artefact of the practice of magic. The Aztec city was built to reflect a sacred cosmogony in which humankind was living in the last of five worlds, or 'Suns'. When the last Sun ceased to shine, the city would be destroyed. Tenochtitlan sheltered those who lived in it from the gods – but only if they tended the city with the utmost care. 'Through the devoted sweeping and ordering of the houses of men and the houses of gods, through remembering the sprinkle of pulque [an alcoholic brew] and the pinch of food routinely offered at the hearthstone, and the daily lacerations to draw forth one's own blood, the Great Ones' destructive manifestations might be held in check.'

For the Aztecs the gods were forces of havoc in the world. Forever at risk of disruption, order was a thin veil stretched over chaos. No increase of knowledge or understanding could deliver human life from primordial disorder.

A belief in underlying chaos lay at the heart of the Aztecs' remarkably delicate aesthetic sensibility. If order was fleeting, so was beauty. Transiency was a mark of what is ultimately real – the opposite of many western traditions in which it is the passing world that lacks substance. The Aztecs used feathers not just as a type of adornment but as a pointer to the nature of things: like human life, the feather-work in which they delighted was essentially transitory. The ritual use of flowers expressed a similar conception. Warriors were taught to seek a 'flowery' death, a willed surrender to mortality that was celebrated in verse.

A belief in underlying chaos underpinned order throughout Aztec society. The violence of the state mirrored that of the cosmos and the gods. The Aztecs felt no shame in making a spectacle of killing. The population rejoiced in 'the lines of victims dragged or driven up the wide steps of the pyramids to meet the waiting priests . . . fêted through the streets, to dance and die before the deities they represented . . . The killings, whether large or small, were frequent: part of the pulse of living.'

Such practices cannot help evoking horror. A way of life based on human slaughter can only be a type of barbarism. But barbarians may have something to teach those who think themselves civilized, and in this case they show how tenuous are the assumptions on which western thinkers base their hopes of peace. Even the greatest realists among these thinkers base their account of order in society on an account of human motivation that is far removed from reality.

Consider Thomas Hobbes. A byword for a hard-boiled view of life – 'Hobbesian' has passed into common use as shorthand for a brutish struggle for survival – the seventeenth-century Enlightenment thinker was able to erect his bold edifice of thought only by excluding actually existing human beings from it.

The system constructed by Hobbes has an impressive simplicity. Aiming to rely on a minimum of morality, he postulated that human beings want to avoid death by violence more than they want anything else. Finding themselves threatened with such a death, they will contract with one another to set up a ruler with unlimited power to command obedience. This sovereign – a mortal god, Hobbes sometimes writes – will bring peace to warring humanity: 'The Passions that encline men to Peace, are Feare of Death; Desire of such things as are necessary to commodious living; and a Hope by their Industry to obtain them. And Reason suggesteth convenient Articles of Peace, upon which men may be drawn to agreement.'

Without this contract, Hobbes declared in a famous passage in Chapter 13 of his book *Leviathan*,

> there is no place for Industry; because the fruit thereof is uncertain; and consequently no Culture of the Earth, no Navigation, nor use of the commodities that may be imported by Sea; no commodious Building; no Instruments of moving, and removing such things as require much force; no Knowledge of the face of the Earth; no account of Time; no Arts; no Letters; no Society; and which is worst of all, continuall feare, and danger of violent death . . .

Rendered in peerless English prose, it is a fine fancy. Much of the later part of Hobbes's long life (he died in 1679 aged ninety-one) was given over to work in geometry – in particular, to squaring the circle. His belief that human beings respond to the threat of violent death by seeking peace is no less quixotic. He does not make clear whether he thought the process he described could ever actually occur. Yet there is no doubt that he believed his ideas could be practically useful, and he expressed the hope that his book would fall into the hands of a prince who would apply its teachings.

But if Hobbes's language is marvellously clear, his thought is highly deceptive. The figures that appear in his system are not human beings, however abbreviated. They are homunculi invented in order to overcome a problem human beings are unable to solve: reconciling the imperatives of peace with the demands of their passions. Hobbes recognized that pride and the pursuit of glory stand in the way of order. Even so he believed that, impelled by the fear of death, humankind could renounce violent conflict and build a lasting peace.

Experience suggests otherwise. Rather than trying to escape violence, human beings more often become habituated to it. History abounds with long conflicts – the Thirty Years' War in early seventeenth-century Europe, the Time of Troubles in Russia, twentieth-century guerrilla conflicts – in which continuous slaughter has been accepted as normal. Famously adaptable, the human animal quickly learns to live with violence and soon comes to find satisfaction in it.

It is true that, when they are weary of killing, human beings very often look for a tyrant to keep them in check. But it is never only a dream of order they are pursuing. A more organized type of blood-letting, often directed in the first instance against minorities – Jews, Roma, gay people, immigrants and others who may seem different – is part of the dream. Instead of passing their days in dull and senseless misery, those who practise persecution can see themselves as players in a struggle between good and evil.

Unable to exorcize violence within themselves, humans have chosen to sanctify it. This – without any pretence or compunction – was the Aztecs' solution to the problem of order. Ritual killing embodied the savagery that is part of any kind of peace among humans.

When the *tlatoani* – the 'Great Speaker' who exercised supreme power – died and passed into the other world, the ruling lineage selected a new ruler from its adult males. Prowess in war was a crucial consideration, but once chosen the new ruler had to be imbued with the qualities of a god. Entering his palace only after a night passed praying naked in front of an image of the god Tezcatlipoca – the god of warriors and sorcerers whose name 'Smoking Mirror' referred to the obsidian mirrors made from dark volcanic glass that were used by the priests for divination – the ruler embodied the fickleness of fate. Also described as 'the mocker', Tezcatlipoca was celebrated in a poem whose first line reads: 'I myself am the enemy.' This was the god who entered into the ruler-elect. At that point the new ruler was possessed and there was no hope of taming his savagery: 'when we replaced one, when we selected someone . . . he was already our lord, our executioner, and our enemy.'

The contrast with western models of authority is stark. Hobbes may have described his absolute sovereign as a mortal god, but it was a god bound by the terms of an agreement: if it did not keep the peace, it could be overthrown. But what if the ruler used its absolute power to pre-empt rebellion and then behaved with the arbitrariness of a god? The Aztecs expected nothing else. No one among them imagined that power could be tamed. But nor did they believe it could be dispensed with. Humans were fated to live in a world in which their rulers were their enemies. Yet these same enemies ensured a type of order that would not otherwise be possible.

If Hobbes had been right in his diagnosis of human conflict, Aztec life could only be a brutish anarchy, without art, industry or letters. The actuality was the thriving metropolis that so amazed the invading Spaniards. Destroyed soon after the conquistadores arrived, the Aztec city was an experimental refutation of some of the most fundamental assumptions of modern western ethics and politics.

Nothing about the Aztecs is as unsettling as their way of death. Many reasons have been suggested for their practice of ritual sacrifice. Clendinnen lists some of these 'grandly simple explanations': 'human sacrifice as a device to enrich a protein-poor diet; human sacrifice as the invention of a sinister and cynical elite, a sort of amphetamines-for-the-people account; human sacrifice as technology, the Mexica response to the second law of thermodynamics, with the taking of the hot and pulsing human heart their despairing effort to replace energy lost by entropic waste'. As she writes, any explanation of this kind 'assumes that which most needs to be demonstrated'.

It may be more useful to look at what happened. The victims were none of them volunteers. They seem to have been mostly outsiders – captives taken in war and slaves received in tribute from other cities. Only one category of victim definitely came from within the community – the small children who were offered to the god at points on the sacred calendar, who had been 'purchased' from their mothers. With regard to adult victims, a variety of techniques was employed to secure compliance. Most likely mind-altering drugs were used along with alcohol, together with practices of rehearsal that numbed the feeling of dread. There was no affectation of sympathy towards the victims. But nor were the victims seen as less than human, like so many casualties of the mass slaughters of the twentieth century, or sacrificed for the sake of an imaginary future generation that would live in peace. Instead, the captor and the captive were merged into one.

At the core of the rituals surrounding the killing was a blurring of the sense of self. Admired by their captors, warrior captives were visited and adorned in preparation for their deaths. Once the captive was killed – whether by ritual combat or by being beheaded on the killing stone at the top of the temple pyramid – the captor was given a gourd of blood, with which he daubed the mouths of idols throughout the city. The flesh of the captive was then used by the captor's family in a ritual meal. But the captor himself did not partake, saying, 'Shall I perchance eat my very self?'

Aiming to loosen the grip of the warrior's conventionally assigned identity, these ritual killings allowed a connection to be made with the chaos that was seen to be more truly real. Stripping away the meanings with which the mind covers its fear, the killings allowed a revelation of naked humanity. Having been exposed, the absence of meaning was once again veiled. Swaddled in blood, life began again.

In Aztec thinking humans do not come into the world as fully functioning beings. Half-finished puppets of the gods, they must make their own identities – but not by choosing who or what they will be. Their 'faces' emerge in interaction with a world they can never control, or come close to understanding.

In the ritual killings, nothing was left of human pride. If they were warriors, the victims were denied any status they had in society. Stripped of their warrior regalia, they were:

> trussed like deer to be lugged, heads lolling, up the pyramid steps; others, similarly trussed, cast writhing into the fire . . . The watchers must have seen an unfluent movement of men, climbing or stumbling or dragged up the steps; then seized, flung back, a priest's arm rising, falling, then rising again; the flaccid bodies rolling and bouncing down the pyramid's flanks . . . They watched again as each broken, emptied cadaver was taken up to be carried to the captor's home temple for dismemberment and distribution: flesh scraped from skulls and thighbones; fragments of flesh cooked and eaten; human skins, dripping with grease and blood, stretched over living flesh; clots of blood scooped up to smear the temple walls.

It must have been a grisly spectacle – and for anyone who reads about it today, it is also uncanny. In Aztec ritual, Clendinnen concludes: '[The Aztecs] knew they were killing their fellow men. It was that humanity which defined them as victims. The Mexica [Aztec] genius, deployed across the astonishing stretch of their ceremonial life, was to figure a human stance within the inhuman conditions of existence.'

It is a superb summation, but it does not remove a sense of unease. The alien quality of the Aztec world does not come simply from the fact that they made a spectacle of killing. The Romans did as much in their gladiatorial games, but they did so for the sake of entertainment. The uncanniness of the Aztecs comes from the fact that they killed in order to create meaning in their lives. It is as if by practising human sacrifice as they did the Aztecs were unveiling something that in our world has been covered up.

Modern humanity insists violence is inhuman. Everyone says nothing is dearer to them than life – except perhaps freedom, for which some assert they would willingly die. Many have been ready to kill on an enormous scale for the sake of creating a future in which no one dies of violence. There are also some convinced that violence is fading away. All say they want an end to the slaughter of humans by other humans that has shaped the course of history.

The Aztecs did not share the modern conceit that mass killing can bring about universal peace. They did not envision any future when humans ceased to be violent. When they practised human sacrifice it was not to improve the world, still less to fashion some higher type of human being. The purpose of the killing was what they affirmed it to be: to protect them from the senseless violence that is inherent in a world of chaos. That human sacrifice was a barbarous way of making meaning tells us something about ourselves as much as them. Civilization and barbarism are not different kinds of society. They are found – intertwined – whenever human beings come together.

If you take the Aztec world seriously – and it was, after all, one made by human beings – you will see the modern world in a new light. Humans kill one another – and in some cases themselves – for many reasons, but none is more human than the attempt to make sense of their lives. More than the loss of life, they fear loss of meaning. There are many who prefer dying to some kinds of survival, and quite a few that have chosen to go to a violent end.

At this point it is easy to think of jihadists courting martyrdom, but not all who choose a violent end are religious believers. Suicide-bombing has often been taken up for pragmatic reasons: it is a cost-effective method in asymmetric warfare, which can have benefits for the bombers' families. But the practice has spread because it appeals to a need for meaning. The Tamil guerrilla fighters in Sri Lanka who first developed the explosive suicide vest were disciples of Lenin, as were some of the suicide-bombers in Lebanon in the Eighties. Rejecting any idea of an afterlife, they cherished the far more absurd fantasy of making a new world.

That humans are prone to absurdity was recognized by Hobbes. In a delightful passage in Chapter 5 of *Leviathan* that undermines much of the rest of the book, he writes of 'the priviledge of Absurdity; to which no living creature is subject, but man only'. By absurdity Hobbes meant the tendency of humans to use words without meaning, and then act on them. Here he pointed to a feature of the human animal that his rationalist philosophy concealed from view. Alone among the animals, humans seek meaning in their lives by killing and dying for the sake of nonsensical dreams. Chief among these absurdities, in modern times, is the idea of a new humanity.

In the twentieth century, the worst episodes of mass killing were perpetrated with the aim of remaking the species. If followers of Lenin dreamt of a socialist humanity, the Nazis imagined they were bringing into being a 'superior race'. Western governments that launch wars of regime change may seem in another league, but the impulses that drive them are not altogether different. Critics claim the true aims of these adventures are geopolitical – the seizure of oil or some other strategic advantage. No doubt geopolitics plays a part, but a type of magical thinking may be more important. Serving no realizable strategic objective, wars of regime change are an attempt to secure a place in history. By intervening in societies of which they know nothing, western elites are advancing a future they believe is prefigured in themselves – a new world based on freedom, democracy and human rights. The results are clear – failed states, zones of anarchy and new and worse tyrannies; but in order that they may see themselves as world-changing figures, our leaders have chosen not to see what they have done.

If the Aztecs also practised a type of magical thinking, they knew that their magic would eventually fail. When the Spaniards came they fitted nowhere in the Aztec scheme. Treacherous and cowardly, they breached every custom of war – attacking unarmed men, killing warriors on sacred ground, wiping out entire villages and kidnapping the *tlatoani*. The invading Spaniards also brought plague with them – the smallpox that ravaged the region's indigenous populations.

Looking for guidance in omens, the Aztecs saw a light in the sky that sank into the lake. Still resisting and enduring a four-month siege, they surrendered only when the last *tlatoani* was caught trying to flee the city. The last of the five Suns had ceased to shine.

The ruin of the city was total. Having described its great rooms, courtyards, orchards, stonework and temples, one of the Spanish soldiers wrote: 'All that I then saw is overthrown and destroyed; nothing is left standing.' The remaining inhabitants were marked by the Spaniards as slaves. Women and boys were branded on the face. Promised safety, the *tlatoani* was tortured and then hanged. The temple guardians were killed by having dogs set on them.

No one can know what the priests thought in their final agony, but it is possible to suppose that they were not surprised by their fate.

DARK MIRRORS, HIDDEN ANGELS AND AN ALGORITHMIC PRAYER-WHEEL

For some advanced thinkers, violence is a type of backwardness. In the more modern parts of the world, they tell us, war has practically disappeared. A litter of semi-failed states, lacking the benefits of modern institutions and modern ideas, the developing world may still be wracked by every kind of conflict – ethnic, tribal and sectarian. Elsewhere humankind has marched on. The great powers are neither internally divided nor inclined to go to war with one another. With the spread of democracy and the increase of wealth, these states preside over an era of peace the like of which the world has never seen. For those who lived through it, the last century may have seemed notably violent; but that is a subjective, unscientific judgement, and not much more than anecdote. Objectively assessed, the number of those killed in violent conflicts was steadily dropping. The numbers are still falling, and there is reason to think they will fall further. A vast shift is under way, not strictly inevitable but still enormously powerful. After many centuries of slaughter, humankind is entering the era of the long peace. Presented with an impressive array of tables and figures, this has proved a popular message.

To be sure, the picture of declining violence may not be all that it seems to be. The statistics that are presented focus heavily on deaths on the battlefield. If these numbers have been falling, one reason is the balance of terror: nuclear weapons have so far prevented industrial-style warfare between great powers. At the same time deaths of non-combatants have been steadily rising. Around a million of the ten million deaths due to the First World War were those of non-combatants. Half of the more than fifty million casualties in the Second World War and over 90 per cent of the millions who have perished in the conflict that has raged in the Congo for decades almost unnoticed by western opinion belong in that category. Again, if great powers have avoided direct armed conflict since the end of the Second World War they have at the same time pursued their rivalries in many proxy wars. Colonial and neo-colonial conflicts in South-East Asia, the Korean War and the Chinese invasion of Tibet, British counter-insurgency warfare in Malaya and Kenya, the abortive Franco-British invasion of Suez, the Angolan civil war, the Soviet invasions of Hungary, Czechoslovakia and Afghanistan, the Vietnam War, the Iran–Iraq War, American involvement in the genocide of indigenous peoples in Guatemala, the first Gulf War, covert intervention in the Balkans and the Caucasus, the invasion of Iraq, the use of airpower in Libya, military aid to insurgents in Syria, the proxy war that is being waged against a background of ethnic divisions in Ukraine – these are only some of the contexts in which great powers have been involved in continuous warfare while avoiding direct conflict with one another.

War has changed, but it has not become less destructive. Rather than a contest between well-organized states that can at some point negotiate peace it is now more often a many-sided conflict among armed irregulars in fractured or collapsed states, which no one has the power to end. The ferocious and seemingly unending conflict in Syria – which features the methodical use of starvation and systematic destruction of urban environments, alongside continuous sectarian massacres – suggests a type of unconventional warfare whose time has come.

Among other casualties, statistics of battlefield deaths pass over the victims of state terror. With increasing historical knowledge it has become clear that the 'Holocaust-by-bullets' – the mass shootings of Jews in Nazi-occupied countries, mostly in the former Soviet Union, during the Second World War – was perpetrated on an even larger scale than previously realized. Soviet agricultural collectivization incurred millions of foreseeable deaths, mainly as a result of starvation, with deportation to uninhabitable regions, life-threatening conditions in the gulag and military-style operations against recalcitrant villages also playing a part. Peacetime casualties of internal repression under the Mao regime have been estimated to be around seventy million. How these deaths fit into the overall scheme of declining violence is unclear.

Estimating the numbers involves complex questions of cause and effect, which cannot always be separated from moral judgements. There are many kinds of lethal force that do not lead to immediate death. Are those who die from hunger or disease during a war or in its aftermath counted among the casualties? Do refugees whose lives are shortened by their sufferings appear in the count? Do victims of torture figure in the calculus if they succumb years later from the physical or mental damage that has been inflicted on them? Do infants who are born to brief and painful lives as a result of exposure to Agent Orange or depleted uranium find a place in the roll call of the dead? If women who have been raped as part of a military strategy of sexual violence die before their time, will their deaths appear in the statistical tables?

While the seeming exactitude of statistics showing a decline in violence has a compelling charm, the human cost of warfare may be incalculable. Deaths by violence are not all equal. It may be terrible to die as a conscript in the trenches or in an aerial bombing campaign. It is worse to be killed as part of a systematic campaign of extermination. Even among the worst kinds of violence there are qualitative differences. To perish from overwork, beating or cold in a labour camp, your end unknown to those who care for you, may be a greater evil than death in battle. It is worse still to be consigned to a camp such as Treblinka, which existed only to deal out death. Passing over these distinctions, the statistics presented by those who celebrate the long peace are morally dubious, if not meaningless.

The highly contingent nature of the figures is another reason for not taking them too seriously. If the Socialist Revolutionary Fanya Kaplan had succeeded in assassinating Lenin when two of the three bullets she fired at him entered his body in August 1918, violence would still have raged in Russia for some years; but the Soviet state might not have survived and the killing machine Lenin went on to construct could not have been used by Stalin for slaughter on a larger scale. If a resolute war leader had not unexpectedly come to power in Britain in May 1940, Europe would most likely have remained under Nazi rule for decades if not generations to come – time in which it could implement more fully its plans of racial purification and genocide. If the Cuban missile crisis had not been defused as the result of action by a single courageous individual – a Soviet submariner who rejected orders from his captain to launch a nuclear torpedo – a nuclear war could have occurred causing colossal numbers of fatalities.

There is something repugnant in the notion that endemic warfare in small and weak states is a result of their backwardness. Desolating some of the most refined civilizations that have ever existed, the wars that ravaged South-East Asia in the Second World War and the decades that followed were the work of colonial powers. One of the causes of the genocide in Rwanda in 1994 was the segregation of the population by German and Belgian imperialism. War in the Congo has been fuelled by western demand for natural resources. If violence has dwindled in advanced societies, one reason may be that they have exported it. Then again, the idea that violence is declining in the most highly developed countries is questionable. Judged by accepted standards, the United States is the most advanced society in the world. It also has the highest rate of incarceration, some way ahead of Mugabe's Zimbabwe. Around a quarter of all the world's prisoners are held in American gaols, many for exceptionally long periods. The state of Louisiana imprisons more of its population per capita than any country in the world – three times as many as Iran, for example. A disproportionate number of the vast American gaol population are black, many prisoners are mentally ill and growing numbers aged and infirm. Imprisonment in America involves the continuous risk of violence from other inmates, including an endemic threat of rape, and months or years spent in solitary confinement – a penalty that has sometimes been classified as torture. Along with mass incarceration, torture appears to be integral in the functioning of the world's most advanced state. It may not be accidental that the practice is often deployed in the special operations that have in many contexts replaced traditional warfare. The extension of counter-terrorism operations to include assassination by unidentifiable mercenaries and remote-controlled killing by the use of drones is part of this shift.

Deaths on the battlefield have declined and may continue to decline. From one angle this can be seen as an advancing condition of peace. From another point of view that looks at the variety and intensity with which violence is being employed, the long peace can be described as a condition of perpetual war.

It is obvious that these are quibbles. Talk of state terror and proxy wars, mass incarceration and torture only dampens the spirit, while questioning the statistics is to miss the point. It is true that the figures are murky, leaving a vast range of casualties unaccounted for. But the human value of these numbers comes from this opacity. Like the obsidian mirrors the Aztecs made from volcanic glass and used for purposes of divination, these rows of graphs and numbers contain nebulous images of an unknown future – visions that by their very indistinctness are capable of giving comfort to anxious believers in human improvement.

Plundered and brought to Europe after the Aztecs were conquered and destroyed by the Spaniards, one of these mirrors was used as a 'scrying-glass' by the Elizabethan mathematician, navigator and magician Dr John Dee (1527–1608/9). In her celebrated study *The Rosicrucian Enlightenment*, first published in 1972, Frances Yates describes Dee as 'a figure typical of the late Renaissance magus who combined "Magia, Cabala, and Alchymia" to achieve a world-view in which advancing science was strangely mingled with angelology'. Described by Queen Elizabeth as 'my philosopher', Dee acted as a court adviser and 'intelligencer' or spy. Travelling widely in Europe, he pursued his interest in science and hermetic philosophy while engaged on other missions.

Dee's fame came from his reputed possession of occult powers. Working with a scryer or medium, he claimed to discern 'angels' pointing to letters and symbols, which he transcribed. According to Dee, the archangel Michael appeared in one of these sessions with a message about the relationship between divine and earthly powers. Commanding Dee to record what he was about to see, the angel produced some elaborate tables, each containing lists of numbers and letters, which together contained a revelation of a future global order based on godly principles. Dee copied the tables into his notebook, and at that point the scryer fell silent.

In his biography of Dee, Benjamin Woolley writes that more than almost anyone at the time Dee realized that the impact of the scientific revolution would be to displace humankind from the centre of things. He:

> had seen with his own eyes the world spill off the edge of the map, and the universe burst out of its shell. And as the cosmos had spread into infinity, so he had seen his and everyone's position in it correspondingly reduced. For the first time in over a thousand years, anyone with the learning to see (and there were still very few) beheld a universe that no longer revolved around the world, and a world that no longer revolved around humans.

The role of occult beliefs in Dee's time was peculiarly modern. The emerging science of astronomy reinforced the appeal of magic as a way of securing human primacy in the world. Like many others in late Renaissance times, Dee needed reassurance of the continuing importance of human action. Offering a vision of the future in their tables of letters and figures, the angels confirmed that humans still had a central place in the cosmos.

Five centuries later, there are many who need reassurance of their significance in the world. The Aztecs and the Elizabethans looked into their mirrors to discern danger. Today those who peer into the future want only relief from anxiety. Unable to face the prospect that the cycles of war will continue, they are desperate to find a pattern of improvement in history. It is only natural that believers in reason, lacking any deeper faith and too feeble to tolerate doubt, should turn to the sorcery of numbers. Happily there are some who are ready to assist them. Just as the Elizabethan magus transcribed tables shown to him by angels, the modern scientific scryer deciphers numerical auguries of angels hidden in ourselves.

To give succour to the spiritually needy is an admirable vocation. No one will deny the intellectual ingenuity and humanistic passion that go into the effort. Still, there is always room for improvement. Whether they are printed on paper or filed on an e-reader, books cannot give the most enlightened among us what they most need: an instantly available sensation of newly created meaning. It is only new inventions that can meet modern needs. At the same time, inspiration can be found in more primitive technologies.

A revolving metal cylinder containing a sacred text, the Tibetan prayer-wheel is set in motion by the turn of a human hand. The result is an automated form of prayer, which the votary believes may secure good fortune and a prospect of liberation from the cycle of birth and death. The belief-system that the prayer-wheel serves may possess a certain archaic charm, with the sacred texts displaying a dialectical subtlety rarely found in western philosophy. Still, it is self-evident to any modern mind that the practice is thoroughly unscientific. How much better, then, to develop a state-of-the-art prayer-wheel – an electronic device containing inspirational texts on the progress of humanity, powered by algorithms that show this progress to be ongoing.

Unlike the old-fashioned prayer-wheel, the device would be based on the best available scientific knowledge, including big data demonstrating the decline of violence. Designed as an amulet or talisman that could be worn at all times, it would have the ability instantly to process and deliver statistics that never fail to show long-term improvement in the human world. If regress of any kind occurred, it would appear as a temporary pause in the forward march of the species. Best of all, the device would be fully interactive. In order to ward off moods of doubt, it could be programmed to broadcast at regular intervals a sound version of the figures. The wearer could recite the statistics out loud, and by constant repetition expel any disturbing thoughts from the mind.

There will be some who object that meaning cannot be manufactured and then programmed into our minds in this way. Meaning shows itself in intimations, these reactionaries will say – the shadow that reminds of mortality; the sudden vista that reveals an unimagined loveliness; the brief glance that opens a new page. Such objections will count for nothing. The advance of knowledge cannot be halted any more than the desire for improvement can be permanently thwarted. A state-of-the-art electronic tablet continuously generating meaning from numbers will render the dark mirrors and prayer-wheels of the past obsolete.

HUMAN REDUNDANCY AND THE CYBORG ECONOMY

The pioneers of modern robotics, Norbert Wiener and John von Neumann, were both involved in the

Manhattan Project which produced the atomic bomb. Wiener is recognized as having originated cybernetics, while Neumann is acknowledged to be the principal progenitor of the mathematical theory of games. They were fully aware that the sciences they were developing opened up possibilities that stretched far beyond the struggle against Nazism. Writing in 1954, Wiener mused on the power that humans were acquiring with this new knowledge:

> [Humans are] playing a game against the arch enemy, disorganization. Is this devil Manichaean or Augustinian? Is it a contrary force opposed to order or is it the very absence of order itself? The difference between these two sorts of demons will make itself apparent in the tactics to be used against them. The Manichaean devil is an opponent, like any other opponent, who is determined on victory and will use any trick of craftiness or dissimulation to obtain this victory. In particular, he will keep his policy of confusion secret, and if we show any signs of beginning to discover his policy, he will change it in order to keep us in the dark. On the other hand, the Augustinian devil, which is not a power in itself, but the measure of our own weakness, may require our full resources to uncover, but when we have uncovered it, we have in a certain sense exorcised it . . .

For Wiener science was a game played against nature. Whether nature was a malign demiurge or a mere absence of order was left open. Even in the latter case nature exhibits a kind of intelligence, and there is no reason to rule out the possibility that machines will do so too. If nature in the form of the human species could bring forth intelligent machines, the process of evolution would continue among the machines.

In 1964, Wiener envisioned such a process:

> Man makes man in his own image. This seems to be the echo or the prototype of the act of creation, by which God is supposed to have made man . . . What is the image of a machine? Can this image, as embodied in one machine, bring a machine of a general sort, not yet committed to a particular specific identity, to reproduce the original machine, either absolutely or under some change that may be construed as a variation?

Could a game be played between humans and machines, the effect of which would be to leave machines beyond the comprehension of their human inventors? Might the process whereby new types of machines developed come to be as much of a mystery as the act of creation in religion? Wiener thought the answer to these questions was 'Yes', and just such a prospect was also envisioned by Neumann:

> It is not unlikely that if you had to build an automaton now you would plan the automaton, not directly, but on some general principles which concern it, plus a machine which could put these into effect, and will construct the ultimate automaton and do it in [such] a way that you yourself don't know any more what the automaton will be.

Towards the end of his life Neumann became preoccupied with the relations of computers with the human mind. An unfinished manuscript published posthumously as *The Computer and the Human Brain* (1958) explored similarities and differences between the two. In a foreword to the third edition of the book, Ray Kurzweil writes that Neumann 'define[s] the essential equivalence of the human brain and a computer'. He declares, 'Artificial intelligence . . . will ultimately soar past unenhanced human thinking.' Kurzweil has no fears regarding this prospect: 'the purpose of this endeavour is not to displace us but to expand the reach of what is already a human-machine civilization.' It is not obvious why Kurzweil is so sure that human purpose will prevail.

The pioneers of robotics were more sceptical. Wiener and Neumann envisaged situations arising when thinking machines could cease to be either controllable or comprehensible by their makers. Implicitly, they recognized that machines would develop by natural selection – a process without purpose or direction. Eventually humans could find themselves displaced by thinking machines they had originally created. The upshot of progress in human knowledge and invention might well be human redundancy.

Kurzweil and other scientific futurists celebrate the increase of knowledge as enhancing human power. By controlling natural processes, they believe, humans can gain mastery of the planet and even the universe. It does not occur to them to inquire who or what will exercise this mastery. Dreaming of a more fully self-aware species, they are attempting to create another version of humankind – one that reflects the flattering image they cherish of themselves as rational beings.

The icons of the prevailing faith in science came into the world as a result of the imperatives of war. Emerging towards the end of the Second World War and developing in the Cold War that followed, the new technologies of robotics and artificial intelligence were tools of human conflict. During the Second World War Wiener suggested that funds be made available for research on computers as part of a project on automatic gun control – an early example of what would prove to be a continuing interaction between war and the rise of computer-controlled machines. Later, Neumann's work in game theory was used to deal with the strategic dilemmas that resulted when the Soviet Union acquired nuclear weapons.

It was not long before the new sciences escaped from what Philip Mirowski, in his study of their role in economics, has described as their 'military incubator'. Theories of computation, information and dynamic systems, which had been confined to engineering and the physical sciences, were applied to the human world. It came to be believed that society could be understood using the same methods that are used to understand machines, and from there it was a small step to think that society is in fact a kind of machine. Long bewitched by the idea of a mathematical model of human behaviour, economists were captivated by the prospect.

As Mirowski writes of the spread of cybernetic thinking into economics in the decades after the Second World War: 'If there was one tenet of that era's particular faith in science, it was that logical rigour and the mathematical idiom of expression would produce transparent agreement over the meaning and significance of various models and their implications.' What cybernetics offered economics was not just the power of prediction and control – though that was certainly part of the appeal of the new science – but the possibility of understanding human behaviour in non-human terms. If the economy could be modelled as a machine, the values and meanings that human beings brought to the market could be discounted. Whether they knew it or not, human actors were incidental to the operation of a system that was more rational than they could ever be. The economy was becoming a computer in which human judgement was superfluous.

Curiously, though perhaps not unpredictably, this vision of the market attracted some who had been enthusiasts for central economic planning. As one of them wrote: 'When I think of it, it's not such a great distance from communist cadre to software engineer. I may have joined the party to further social justice, but a deeper attraction could have been to a process, a system, a program. I'm inclined to think I've always believed in the machine.' For former communists as for those who had never questioned the free market, the idea that the economy was a highly sophisticated machine was irresistible. Human labour would continue to be necessary. But with their mercurial passions and irrational longings, human beings were obstacles to the machine's efficient functioning.

A few decades later it is no longer clear that the machine needs large inputs of human labour. Many have observed how the internet has decimated some industries and fundamentally altered others. As banking, the allocation of capital in markets, medical diagnostics and many managerial functions are automated, whole swaths of professional occupations seem close to being wiped out. It is not just the superior computational powers of computers that are eliminating these jobs. The developing capacity for pattern-recognition is displacing human judgement.

Unskilled labour is being automated, while many functions that have been assumed to require human contact will no longer do so. Robot nurses and teachers, sex workers and soldiers are ceasing to be merely the stuff of speculative fiction. If these replacements for human labour are not yet feasible, it is likely that they soon will be. Self-driving cars and telephones that interact with human voices are the front line of a rapidly advancing trend. Occupations that seemed safe because they required a level of skill or education are no longer secure.

There is no reason to expect technological innovation to stop or slow. As we are forever being reminded, the advance of knowledge is now an exponential process. Some believe computers will soon pass the Turing test – named after the great mathematician who played a vital role breaking German codes at Bletchley Park during the Second World War – and display intelligent behaviour indistinguishable from that of humans. Kurzweil may well be right in his forecast that within a decade or so computers will be joking and flirting with their users.

Economists may object that in the past technological innovation has not reduced employment permanently – as old occupations have died out, others have been born. But robotic technologies are unparalleled in their scope and reach. If an earlier burst of technological advance left behind a lumpenproletarian underclass, the current wave looks set to create a lumpenbourgeoisie. Denied any prospect of a lifelong career, lacking pensions or savings, the former middle classes can expect a life of precarious insecurity for the foreseeable future. A few may recreate the trappings of Edwardian privilege, but for most a bourgeois life of any kind will soon be as remote as feudalism.

The inherent tendency of this wave of technological innovation seems to be to render the human majority superfluous in the process of production. In a more remote future envisioned by techno-enthusiasts, human redundancy could be more complete. There is no way even a small elite will be able to keep up with the development of artificial intelligence. In the longer run the only rational course of action will be to reconstruct the humans that remain so that they more closely resemble machines. A technologically enhanced species will join in in the ongoing evolutionary advance. As for the remnants that are left behind, human obsolescence is a part of progress.

AN IRON MOUNTAIN AND A SHIFTING SPECTACLE

A visionary study first published anonymously in 1967 presented a new paradigm of social order: 'War is not, as is widely assumed, primarily an instrument of policy utilized by nations to extend or defend their expressed political values or their economic interests. On the contrary, it is itself the principal basis of organization on which all modern societies are constructed.' The study recognized a fact not addressed in mainstream thinking: the constant threat of war is one of the essential features of the modern state. 'The historical record', it notes, 'reveals one instance after another where the failure of a regime to maintain the credibility of a war threat led to its dissolution ... The organization of a society for the possibility of war is its principal political stabilizer.'

But it is not just political authority that requires the threat of war. So does the organization of society as a whole:

> In advanced modern democratic societies, the war system has provided political leaders with another political-economic function of increasing importance: it has served as the last great safeguard against the elimination of necessary social classes. As economic productivity increases to a

> level further and further above that of minimum subsistence, it becomes more and more difficult for a society to maintain distribution patterns insuring the existence of 'hewers of wood and drawers of water'. The further progress of automation can be expected to differentiate still more sharply between 'superior' workers and what Ricardo called 'menials', while simultaneously aggravating the problem of maintaining an unskilled labor supply.

The problems of political authority and social stability the study identified in the Sixties are more pressing today. How can order be maintained when 'superior' workers comprise only a small fraction of the population and much of the population is composed of 'menials' whose services are no longer needed? How could a society in which the majority has no productive role possibly be sustainable?

Having detailed the essential social and political functions that war has provided in the past, the analysis concludes with a number of suggestions for policy-makers:

> – optimum levels of armament production, for purposes of economic control, at any given series of chronological points and under any given relationship between civilian production and consumption patterns;

– correlation factors between draft recruitment policies and mensurable social dissidence;
– minimum levels of population destruction necessary to maintain war-threat credibility under varying political conditions;
– optimum cyclical frequency of 'shooting' wars under varying circumstances of historical relationship.

Claiming to emanate from a 'Special Study Group' with links to the Pentagon and the White House, *Report from Iron Mountain* became a major success. Some readers may have been horrified, but more were intrigued. Seemingly revealing a type of thinking that prevailed in the innermost recesses of the defence establishment, the 'realist' analysis presented in the report had reverberations decades later.

In the Eighties a far-right group distributed thousands of copies without seeking copyright permission. When the author sued the group, its defence was that the book was a government document and therefore not subject to copyright. By the Nineties the report was being used by the Michigan Militia and other far-right American armed groups as 'a sort of bible'. Former Chief of Special Operations under President Kennedy Fletcher Prouty, who came to believe that Kennedy's assassination had been part of a *coup d'état* and achieved celebrity by being the model for

'Mr X' in Oliver Stone's film *JFK* (1991), declared the report 'the real McCoy' and seems to have held this view up to his death in 2001.

Report from Iron Mountain was, of course, a hoax. In 1972 the writer Leonard C. Lewin identified himself as the author in the *New York Times*. By mimicking the jargon-ridden style of think-tanks and government agencies, Lewin was able to convince many readers of the existence of his 'Special Study Group'. Some of them were ready to act on the basis that the group and its plans were fact. Like the mysterious encyclopaedia detailing an alternate planet that features in Borges's 'Tlön, Uqbar, Orbis Tertius', Lewin's fiction became part of the real world.

While Lewin meant his report as satire, it can be read as prophecy. To be sure, the picture of an inner cabal of strategic thinkers directing the course of government has no resemblance to reality. Wracked by internal conflicts, guided by unreliable impressions of volatile and nebulous public moods, seizing on one faddish notion after another, modern governments often have no clear picture of what they are doing, let alone of its unintended consequences. Most likely nothing like the Special Study Group ever existed. If it did, it had no leverage over events. Yet something like the state of affairs that is pictured in the report could have come into being through a process of evolutionary change.

War no longer has some of the functions that the report identifies. Large conscript armies have been abolished in nearly all advanced countries, and drones are further reducing the need for human soldiers. Also, the economic functions of warfare have altered since the report was written. While institutions devoted to intelligence and surveillance are expanding, the military-industrial complex no longer has the centrality it once did. The Reagan administration may have attempted a version of 'military Keynesianism' – the practice of stimulating economic activity through increased defence spending. But with the shrinkage of the defence sector, war no longer generates these benefits.

The role of war in advanced societies now lies elsewhere. Twenty-four-hour news media generate a chronic state of low-intensity anxiety together with a tranquillizing sense of security. Shaping a perception of the world as endemically dangerous, a landscape of terror can be projected anywhere via television screens, laptops and mobile devices. This landscape frames the view of the world, while those who inhabit it are enclosed in a zone of safety. More than on any other single factor, the stability of advanced societies depends on how perceptions are shaped by the media.

In the same year that *Report from Iron Mountain* appeared, Guy Debord's *Society of the Spectacle* was published in France. Bringing together elements from Surrealism, Marxism and anarchism, the book made a mark at a time when student rebellion was under way in Europe and the United States. Much of Debord's analysis was a reworking of familiar and discredited ideas. There is nothing of interest in his fantasies of revolution or in the Marxian schema he deploys to support them.

Yet in one key respect Debord was ahead of his time. The core of advanced capitalism, he suggested, was the creation of a spectacle through which social relationships are mediated. More than simply producing images, the spectacle assigns roles and ambitions to the population. As capitalism has developed, the division of labour in society has become more fluid. No one can rely on having any particular type of employment, and the idea that work can be a means to self-realization is increasingly unreal. In these circumstances it becomes necessary to remotivate the population. With automation advancing rapidly, there may be a decreasing need for human beings in the productive process. It is the need to continue consuming that is central to the economy. Hence the culture of celebrity, which by offering anyone fifteen minutes of fame reconciles everyone to the boredom in which they must pass the rest of their lives.

Debord writes:

> It is in these conditions that a parodic end of the division of labour suddenly appears, with carnivalesque gaiety . . . A financier can be a singer, a lawyer a police spy, a baker can parade his literary tastes, an actor can be president, a chef can philosophise on cookery techniques as if they were landmarks in universal history. Anyone can join the spectacle, in order publicly to adopt, or sometimes secretly practise, an entirely different activity from whatever specialism first made their name. Where 'media status' has acquired infinitely more importance than the value of anything one might actually be capable of doing, it is normal for this status to be readily transferable; for anyone, anywhere, to have the same right to the same kind of stardom.

When he identified the indispensable role of the virtual world created by the media in reproducing the most highly developed varieties of capitalism, Debord grasped one of the ruling facts of the age.

At the time he first published the book, Debord may have believed that his analysis could have a political impact. Simply to reveal the spectacle's workings, he may have thought, would somehow derail it. If so he failed to take into account the fact that knowledge can always be used for a variety of ends. Whether he was surprised when a disciple who became head of Silvio Berlusconi's media empire announced that he had learnt his craft from Debord's writings cannot be known; but the ironic subversion of his thinking must have left a mark.

When the student movement of 1968 failed to trigger a general insurrection, Debord left Paris and spent most of the rest of his life in the French countryside playing war games and drinking. Dissolving the group he had founded – the Situationist International, a fractious claque of some thirty people all of whom he would eventually expel – he retreated into a life of seclusion with his companion Alice Becker-Ho.

Debord committed suicide in 1994. Two of his friends killed themselves shortly afterwards. Both had been acquainted with Debord's publisher and patron, who had been murdered ten years earlier. Debord had written – and possibly boasted – that since the early Seventies he had been under surveillance by the French secret service. Rumours of dark plots were rife. But the cause of his death was almost certainly simpler and more prosaic. Believing his ideas to be without influence and suffering from neurological symptoms of his alcoholism, he had no further use for his life.

By the time he killed himself Debord had come to think the spectacle was indestructible. A society in which it had reached its full development, he writes in a commentary on his original ideas that he published in 1988, displays five mutually reinforcing features: 'incessant technological renewal; integration of state and economy; generalised secrecy; unanswerable lies; an eternal present'. Taken together, these features removed any possibility of revolutionary change.

Clearly, no human institution could possess the power Debord ascribed to the spectacle. Even if today it is near-omnipotent, why are those who live under it so compliant? If human beings could in some way penetrate the ever-present veil, he believed, they would demand a life that was not mediated and distorted. But what if many prefer a vicarious existence in the virtual world?

A self-proclaimed follower of Machiavelli and Sun Tzu, Debord thought of himself as a pitiless realist. Had he ever possessed power, he would surely have been pitiless in exercising it – in the first instance, against those who had been his friends. His capacity for realistic thinking is more questionable. Like revolutionaries everywhere, he believed that the mass of human beings shared his values. He could not conceive that others would not want to be as he imagined he would himself like to be.

It is doubtful whether Debord would have appreciated the joke when in 2009 he was appointed a national treasure by the minister of culture in the government of Nicolas Sarkozy. Intervening to prevent Yale University acquiring Debord's archive, the minister described him as 'one of the last great French intellectuals'. For all his sardonic wit, deficient in any sense of the absurd, he would have regarded his posthumous respectability as final proof that opposition to the spectacle had ceased to be possible.

An abstract entity, 'the spectacle' does not exist. By attributing omnipotence to a theoretical category, Debord showed he had lost any sense of reality. But something would come into being in the decades after his death that exercised some of the functions he attributed to the spectacle. Writing in 1988, he noted the expanding role of secrecy in advanced capitalist societies:

> Our society is built on secrecy, from the 'front' organisations which draw an impenetrable screen over the concentrated wealth of their members, to the 'official secrets' which allow the state a vast field of operation free from any legal constraint; from the often frightening secrets of *shoddy production* hidden by advertising, to the projections of an extrapolated future, in which domination alone reads off the likely progress of things whose existence it denies . . .

Foreseeing the rise of a society based on secrecy, Debord failed to anticipate how new technology would enable the abolition of privacy. Nearly everything that is done leaves an electronic trace, which can be collected and stored indefinitely. It is not only the governments of western states that have the power to monitor the population. So do business corporations, tyrannical states and global networks of organized crime. If western governments were to renounce surveillance, the practice would not cease. Other states and other forces would go on prying and eavesdropping.

The rise of the surveillance state is an integral aspect of globalization. The more fragmented world that existed in the past was more stable than the interconnected world that exists at present, partly because shocks in any part of it were not instantly transmitted to the rest as they are today. This vanished world was also friendlier to privacy. When people are locked into local communities they are subject to continuous informal monitoring of their behaviour. Modern individualism tends to condemn these communities because they repress personal autonomy. But societies that pride themselves on their devotion to freedom dread disorder. The informal controls on behaviour that exist in a world of many communities are unworkable in a world of highly mobile individuals, so society turns to the technology of surveillance. Closed-circuit cameras replace oversight by families and neighbours, while information on the entire population is available on the web. Near-ubiquitous technological monitoring is a consequence of the decline of cohesive societies that has occurred alongside the rising demand for individual freedom.

A degree of privacy may survive as a luxury good. Encrypting parts of their lives, the rich may contrive for themselves a freedom that many people possessed without such effort in the past. For the rest, loss of privacy is the price of individualism. Anyone can achieve a momentary fame, but for nearly everyone today fifteen minutes of anonymity has become an impossible dream.

A UNIVERSAL PANOPTICON

An early version of the surveillance society can be found in a model penitentiary designed by the English Utilitarian philosopher Jeremy Bentham (1748–1832). A singular personality who thought of himself as being above all else rational, Bentham had a penchant for inventing neologisms. Among the hundreds of new words he coined, *international*, *bicameral*, *maximize* and *minimize* are some that have entered everyday use. Others such as 'cacotopia' (Bentham's neologism for a thoroughly undesirable state of society of the sort that would later be described as dystopian) and 'uranoscopic physiurgics' (more widely known as astronomy) have failed to catch on.

The provisions Bentham made for his cadaver reveal his sense of what a rational human being might be like. Leaving instructions that the body be used for dissection, he specified that an 'auto-icon' be constructed from the skeleton and head. Dressed in Bentham's clothes and with a waxen head, a life-sized manikin was created. Passing into the hands of University College London, the doll-like effigy has been on almost continuous public display ever since.

For many years convinced that a rational society could best be constructed under the direction of an enlightened despot, Bentham corresponded with a number of European monarchs. Bentham's brother Samuel visited Russia in order to build a circular textile factory whose overseers could monitor workers without being seen. Bentham joined Samuel in the hope of persuading Catherine the Great to build what he described as a Panopticon (in Greek, 'all-seeing').

As outlined in letters he wrote while he was in Russia, the Panopticon was a multi-storeyed circular building designed so that those who were enclosed within it could be watched at all times. Inmates would be unable to see the central tower and could not know whether they were being watched or not. Each held in a separate cell, they would also be unable to see or communicate with each other. The windows of the observation tower would have venetian blinds, which could be adjusted so that the prisoners would be unable to see shadows. Small lamps backed by reflectors would be installed outside each window, throwing light into the corresponding cell.

Never sure whether they could be seen, the inmates would be compelled to act on the basis that any act of transgression would be witnessed: as Bentham put it, the prisoners would have a constant sense of omnipresence. In order that guards could communicate with each prisoner without others hearing, a tin tube would connect each cell with the observation area. Otherwise silence would be imposed; any noise the prisoners made would be punished by gagging.

The central hall of the building would be intersected by partitions, with each quarter of the hall divided from the rest by zigzag openings rather than doors. In the Panopticon there would be no night; everything would occur in the all-seeing light of the inspector's lamps. With each prisoner cut off from view from every other, they would spend their time in a place that was at once completely closed and entirely open to view, and from which there would be no possibility of escape.

Bentham stipulated that the Panopticon be managed on a contractual basis, with the governor having a direct pecuniary interest in the efficiency of the institution. He was insistent that the institution be self-financing and profit-making, and made clear that forced labour was necessary for this to be possible. If they wished to avoid perpetual solitary confinement on a diet of bread and water, the inmates would have to work. He was conscious that there might be a risk of contractors neglecting the wellbeing of the inmates. To deal with this contingency he proposed that contractors be charged ten pounds for each prisoner who died under their care.

Worked out in obsessive detail, the Panopticon is an example of the cult of reason in action. For Bentham the Panopticon was much more than an ideal prison. The design principles of the penitentiary applied to all social institutions, such as poor-houses, factories, hospitals, mad-houses and schools. In effect the Panopticon was a model for a world in which universal surveillance would be the basis of social control.

Despite Bentham's large ambitions for it and the close attention he gave to its design, nothing like the Panopticon has been built. It may be that the scheme was never cost-effective. Where prisons have been handed over to private companies, omnipresent surveillance of the kind Bentham prescribed has proved to be an unnecessary expense. Sanctions such as solitary confinement, together with the need to deal with violence from other inmates, seem to be sufficient to maintain order.

The situation alters when a Panopticon can be constructed that encloses the entire population. To a large extent, this has already been done. With new technologies of surveillance, economies of scale overcome problems of cost. Since all their electronic communications can be accessed, it is no longer necessary to segregate the inmates from one another. As there is no outside world, escape becomes unimaginable. Technological progress has brought into being a system of surveillance more far-reaching than any Bentham could have conceived.

Enclosing the entire population in a virtual Panopticon might seem the ultimate invasion of freedom. But universal confinement need not be experienced as a privation. If they know nothing else, most are likely to accept it as normal. If the technology through which surveillance operates also provides continuous entertainment, they may soon find any other way of living intolerable.

Alongside the system of surveillance there is a world of media images in which terror and entertainment are intermingled. Seemingly safer than the world outside and more stimulating than unmediated everyday life, this virtual environment resembles the settings of reality television more than it does a prison. A feature of reality shows is that the inmates have nothing to do. Aside from overcoming cleverly staged challenges and interacting emotionally with one another, they are completely idle. It may not be too far-fetched to see in their condition an intimation of the future for the majority of people. If the advance of smart machines leaves most human beings an economic role only as consumers, this may be how they will be expected to pass their time.

One of the strengths of such a universal Panopticon is that the perils against which it protects are not all imaginary. The atrocity exhibitions that are on display in the media are not just fantasies. The most savage wars rage unabated; random violence can happen anywhere at any time. With the rapid evolution of techniques of cyber-attack, every modern amenity is vulnerable to sudden disruption. To assume that the inmates yearn to escape the universal Panopticon would be rash. Their worst fear may be of being forced to leave.

PUPPETRY, CONSPIRACY AND OUIJA BOARDS

In his account of the kidnapping and murder of the Italian Prime Minister Aldo Moro, the Sicilian writer Leonardo Sciascia tells the reader that when he finished putting the documents surrounding the events into some kind of order he could not help thinking of one of Borges's fables. The story was 'Pierre Menard, Author of the *Quixote*' (1941), in which Borges imagines a French writer who, in addition to his little-known oeuvre, writes an altogether unknown masterpiece: a version of *Don Quixote* in which not a word had been changed. What is astonishing in Menard's achievement is not that he wrote the same book again but that he wrote another book. The book was different because the reader was different – starting with Menard himself.

When examining records of the kidnapping, Sciascia writes:

> one had the irresistible impression that the Moro affair had already been written, was already a completed literary work, already existed in all its unbearable perfection. Inviolable except in the manner of Pierre Menard – by changing everything without changing anything . . . Why does the Moro affair give that impression of something already written, something inhabiting a sphere of intangible literary perfection, something that can only be faithfully rewritten and, while being rewritten, be totally altered without altering anything?

The public facts that produced what came to be known as the Moro affair can be quickly recounted. On the morning of 16 March 1978 a group claiming allegiance to the Red Brigades seized Moro while he was being driven to parliament, killing all of his five bodyguards. While being held by the group he underwent trial by a 'people's court' in the course of which he disclosed the role of Italian intelligence agencies in bombings attributed to the neo-fascist right. Fifty-five days after he had been kidnapped, his bullet-riddled body was found in the back of a car in the centre of Rome.

Five times prime minister, Moro had led the Christian Democratic Party towards a 'historic compromise' with the Italian communist party. Occurring in the era of the Cold War, his abduction and execution were interpreted as part of a covert struggle between the superpowers. From the start there were suggestions of conspiracy.

In his book *Puppetmasters: The Political Use of Terrorism in Italy*, the investigative journalist Philip Willan quotes an unnamed secret service officer in an interview with *La Repubblica* newspaper two days after the kidnapping describing the operation as 'so perfect as to seem almost artistic'. Executed by people who 'have undergone lengthy commando training in specialized bases' and directed by an organization that was extremely competent 'both in its genuinely ideologically motivated members and in the sectors that are controlled by other directors, for other purposes, which paradoxically coincide', the operation was not the work of the Red Brigades alone. The implication is that it was an intervention by covert state agencies, though the provenance of these agencies is left open.

Many stories were told in the aftermath of the murder. Some linked Moro's death with Operation Gladio, an underground organization set up by the Allies after the end of the Second World War to promote resistance in the event of a communist coup. Others focused on Moro having information relating to banking scandals involving the Mafia and the Vatican. Most of these stories treated the murder as confirming the existence of a 'parallel government' in Italy, independent of democratic institutions and capable of undermining or bypassing them. With few exceptions, those who have written on the subject have viewed the idea that the kidnapping and murder were committed by those who actually claimed responsibility for the crime as too far-fetched to be worth pursuing.

The affair included some comically absurd episodes. One involved Romano Prodi, a bumbling, avuncular academic who would go on to become head of the vast Institute for Industrial Reconstruction (IRI), Italian prime minister in 1996 and president of the European Commission. On a wet Sunday afternoon in April 1978, while Moro was being held by his captors, Prodi visited the country home of one of his professorial colleagues at the University of Bologna. Having nothing better to do, Prodi and seven of his colleagues decided to while away the afternoon by conducting a seance. Arranging themselves around the Ouija board, they called up the spirit of a dead Christian Democratic politician and asked where Moro was being held. Via the board, the spirit responded. The word 'Gradoli' was slowly spelt out. The name was not known to him or his colleagues, Prodi told the commission inquiring into Moro's death some years later. But they found a village with that name in an atlas, and in the following days the information was passed on to the police. The village was raided and nothing found. Later it appeared that Moro had been held in an apartment in a block of flats in a street in the suburbs of Rome called Via Gradoli. It was from there that he had been taken, before being shot and his body left in the car boot in central Rome.

Prodi's account of receiving the information at a seance was a story few found credible. Many believed he had been tipped off as to Moro's whereabouts and had fabricated the seance in order to protect his source. Others speculated that Prodi's motive could have been to prevent Moro's place of captivity from being identified. Some even suspected that the story of the seance was nothing but a joke.

From one observer the Moro affair evoked something like a theory of terrorism. A member of Debord's Situationist International and the last to be expelled from the organization, Gianfranco Sanguinetti, viewed terrorist activity as a strategy practised by states against their own citizens in a time when these states were losing legitimacy. As a central part of the 'spectacle' – the system of images manufactured through the media to mask real social conditions – terror was being stage-managed:

> in solemnly taking it upon itself to stage the spectacle of the common and sacrosanct defence against the terrorist monster, and in the name of this holy mission, [the state] can exact from all its subjects a further portion of their tiny freedom, which will reinforce police control over the entire population . . . Terrorism and 'the emergency', a state of perpetual emergency and 'vigilance', these are the only existing problems, or at the very least, the only ones which it is permitted and necessary to be preoccupied with. All the rest does not exist, or is forgotten and in any case is silenced, distanced, repressed in the social unconscious, in the face of the gravity of the question of 'public order'.

Sanguinetti's book distinguished between 'offensive' and 'defensive' terrorism, the former being directed against the state and the latter controlled by the state. It goes on to make another distinction between 'direct' terrorist operations – such as neo-fascist attacks on the general population – and 'indirect' operations such as those of the Red Brigades, which strengthen the state by creating a climate of fear. All of these types of terrorism, the book maintains, are covertly directed by states against their own populations.

Sanguinetti's slim volume was first published in Italian in April 1979. He had been imprisoned in 1975 for 'subversive conspiracy', one of the charges against him being that he belonged to the organization that had inspired the Red Brigades. It was a bizarre accusation, and also heavily ironic. The Situationist International had been dissolved in 1972. Its ideas had a wide and enduring influence, but only in the media and fashion – that is to say, within the world that has been created by the spectacle. Few ideas have been more readily co-opted by capitalism.

In his book Sanguinetti claimed that terrorism is sponsored by states against their own populations. This had not always been his view. In letters to Guy Debord in 1978, he suggested that the murder of Moro was what it seemed to be – the work of a genuine revolutionary group, which he appears to have regarded as misguided in its tactics but sound in its view of society. Debord on the other hand always believed that both the Red Brigades and far-right terrorists were directed by the state.

Debord may have been right in thinking that the Italian state had a hand in right-wing and left-wing terrorism. Power never resides only in publicly visible institutions. Much that occurred in these years may have been the work of covert agencies. But this does not mean that what happened was orchestrated. No one directed the crimes that were committed – or fully understood how they came about. Even for the protagonists, the pattern of events must have been indecipherable.

The belief that there is some hidden cabal directing the course of events is a type of anthropomorphism – a way of finding agency in the entropy of history. If someone is pulling the strings behind the stage the human drama is not without meaning. Human beings are not – as they might appear to an impartial spectator – repeatedly trapped in intractable dilemmas: they are puppets of occult forces. This is the message of the *Protocols of the Elders of Zion*, the notorious anti-Semitic forgery fabricated in the last years of the nineteenth century, most likely by the head of the foreign branch of the Tsarist intelligence service. The view of the world expressed in the *Protocols* is entirely delusional, and no doubt for that reason has proved vastly influential. As Norman

Cohn writes, 'what is really important about the *Protocols* is the great influence which – incredibly yet incontestably – they have exercised on twentieth-century history.'

Interpreting history as the work of a conspiracy is a backhanded compliment to human rationality. It assumes a category of people that is capable not only of controlling events but also – and more importantly – of understanding why they occur. But the fundamental problem of conspiracy theories is the same as that which faces conspirators themselves: no one can know why human events happen as they do. History abounds in conspiracies; but none has ever escaped the universal drift of which they form part.

One of the most ingenious conspiracy theories was developed by the twentieth century's greatest authority on scepticism. In *The Second Oswald*, the distinguished philosopher Richard H. Popkin argued that the official account of the Warren Commission in which the assassination of John Kennedy in November 1963 was the work of a lone gunman is marred by too many omissions and inconsistencies to be plausible. Attempting to remedy these defects, he proposed an alternative theory: looking very much like the suspect Lee Harvey Oswald, a second Oswald impersonated the suspect in ways that would distract attention from what had actually happened – the assassination of Kennedy by two other gunmen.

Popkin does not pronounce on the objectives the assassination was meant to achieve. In a 1983 Post-script to *The Second Oswald*, a study of the assassination first published in 1966, he lists eight possibilities that 'are supportable by evidence, and are not disprovable': the true target of the assassination was someone else, and Kennedy was an innocent bystander; the assassination was designed by anti-Castro Cubans, with the aim of precipitating another invasion of Cuba that would achieve what the Bay of Pigs invasion had failed to achieve in 1961; the assassination was conceived and executed by elements in the Mafia because Kennedy and his brother the US attorney general Robert Kennedy were threatening to curb Mafia operations; the assassination was linked with Oswald's Russian involvements, his calm demeanour after being arrested suggesting he was acting as the agent of some branch of Soviet or American intelligence or both; the assassination was planned and carried out by Soviet agents; the assassination was committed so that Soviet agents would be held responsible for it; the assassination was sponsored by Fidel Castro in retaliation for American attempts to assassinate him; or the assassination occurred as part of an internal struggle between rival factions in the CIA.

The list is not meant to be exhaustive, nor are the theories mutually exclusive. But Popkin never doubted that the author of the assassination could in principle be known: 'these are possible scenarios, supported by some evidence and not presently refutable. There are no doubt other scenarios that meet these conditions. Unless more evidence, a confession or two, some secret papers released, somebody's secret memoirs turn up, we may be left at this point.' No doubt he was right in thinking that the Warren Commission's account of the assassination was unsatisfactory. But whatever facts the report may have omitted or covered up, the reason the report was inadequate was not that it failed to finger who was responsible for the crime.

For all his scepticism, Popkin seems to have believed that human events cannot be without meaning; behind the scenes, someone must be in control. There is another possibility, though. Human beings act, certainly. But none of them knows why they act as they do. There is a scattering of facts, which can be known and reported. Beyond these facts are the stories that are told. Human beings may behave like puppets, but no one is pulling the strings. Someone pulled the trigger and shot Kennedy. That does not mean they knew on whose behalf they were acting, or why Kennedy was killed. By the time of the assassination, many actors may have been in play; any plans they may have formed would long ago have been lost in the chaos of events. If they asked themselves why things turned out as they did, the conspirators – if any existed – could only tell stories, like everyone else.

With his intimate knowledge of the labyrinthine deceptions of Sicilian life, Leonardo Sciascia could not help reading the reports of Moro's abduction and murder as accounts of events that had been scripted and staged. Like the reader of Menard's *Quixote*, Sciascia felt a shock of recognition. But if the reported events were staged it was not by a secret author. The author was the reader, who looked at the events and found a story.

We think we have some kind of privileged access to our own motives and intentions. In fact we have no clear insight into what moves us to live as we do. The stories we tell ourselves are like the messages that appear on Ouija boards. If we are authors of our lives, it is only in retrospect.

WHEN THE MACHINE STOPS

'She had never known silence, and the coming of it nearly killed her – it did kill many thousands of people outright. Ever since her birth she had been surrounded by the steady hum. It was to the ear what artificial air was to the lungs, and agonizing pains shot across her head. And scarcely knowing what she did, she stumbled forward and pressed the unfamiliar button, the one that opened the door of her cell.'

The woman is Vashti, the central character in E. M. Forster's story 'The Machine Stops'. Passing her life like everyone else, in an underground cell that provides for all her needs, Vashti has no interest in the natural world:

> There were buttons and switches everywhere – buttons to call for food, for music, for clothing. There was the hot-bath button, by pressure of which a basin of (imitation) marble rose out of the floor, filled to the brim with a warm deodorized liquid. There was the cold-bath button. There was the button that produced literature. And there were of course the buttons by which she communicated with her friends. The room, though it contained nothing, was in touch with all she cared for in the world.

Human life is no longer shaped by the rhythms of the planet. 'Night and day, wind and storm, tide and earthquake, impeded man no longer. He had harnessed Leviathan. All the old literature, with its praise of Nature, and its fear of Nature, rang false as the prattle of a child.' But human relationships could still perturb the calm, and Vashti is worried about her son Kuno. Using a tablet provided by the Machine that enables them to see images of each other, he has told her of his strange desire to see the stars from the surface of the Earth. Boarding an air-ship left over from former times, she travels to see him.

On the way she is disturbed by light coming in from the cabin windows. 'When the air-ships had been built, the desire to look direct at things still lingered in the world. Hence the extraordinary number of skylights and windows, and the proportionate discomfort to those who were civilized and refined. Even in Vashti's cabin one star peeped through a flaw in the blind, and after a few hours' uneasy slumber, she was disturbed by an unfamiliar glow, which was the dawn.' When she swerves away from the sunbeams, the cabin attendant tries to steady her. Vashti is enraged and cries out angrily. 'People never touched one another. The custom had become obsolete, owing to the Machine.' The attendant apologizes for not having let Vashti fall.

When Vashti and Kuno meet they cannot understand one another. He tells her he was unable to obtain an 'Egression-permit' to visit the surface of the planet, so found a way there on his own. She is horrified by this breach of regulations, while he responds by accusing her of worshipping the Machine and thinking him irreligious for finding his own way. 'At this she grew angry. "I worship nothing!" she cried. ". . . I don't think you are irreligious, for there is no such thing as religion left. All the fear and the superstition that existed once have been destroyed by the Machine."' Vashti fears for her son. If he persists in his rebellion, he will suffer the ultimate punishment – expulsion from the Machine.

Vashti and her son part company, and she resumes her eventless existence in her cell. But the Machine was overreaching itself and starting to break down. To begin with, the change was not obvious. The Central Committee that supervised the Machine reported signs of malfunction, and made some adjustments. No one questioned the Machine's powers. Religion had been re-established with the Machine as the Supreme Being. Everyone yielded to 'some invincible pressure, which came no one knew whither, and which, when gratified, was succeeded by some new pressure equally invincible. To such a state of affairs it is convenient to give the name of progress.'

Time passed. The Machine was getting out of hand, but most people adapted to its whims. Vashti's son, with whom she is in contact using the tablet, has told her, 'The Machine stops.' She cannot grasp what he means; the prospect is unthinkable. But mechanical faults were creeping in: the air was becoming dark and foul. Panic started to spread, with people praying to the books that recorded the Machine's omnipotence. New 'nerve-centres' were evolving, they believed, which would do the work of the Machine more efficiently. 'But there came a day when, without any previous hint of feebleness, the entire communication-system broke down, all over the world, and the world, as they had understood it, ended.'

Finally leaving her cell, she finds her fellow inhabitants of the underground city in panic and despair. 'People were crawling about, people were screaming, whimpering, gasping for breath, touching each other, vanishing in the dark . . . Some were fighting round the electric bells, trying to summon trains which could not be summoned . . . Others stood at the doors of their cells fearing, like herself, either to stop in them or to leave them, and behind all the uproar was silence – the silence which is the voice of the earth and of the generations who have gone.'

Published in 1909, Forster's story describes humankind living within a machine. When the machine comes to a stop, it is because its internal workings have become faulty. Like H. G. Wells's *Time Machine* (1895) – by which Forster's was surely influenced – it is a vivid and arresting tale. Where Forster's story loses force is in its failure to explain how the Machine came to have dominion in the first place.

The lack of realism in the story comes from the absence of any serious human conflict. When the Machine start to run down there is discontent; there is some mention of riots. But no Machine that ruled the world as Forster's did could achieve such power without tumultuous revolutions and long wars. Omitting to explain how the Machine achieved its dominance, Forster fails to explain why it broke down. A fault in the works does not take the reader very far. We are left with the enigma of a world inexplicably pacified, which comes suddenly to a standstill.

If the Machine were to stop today, the most likely cause would be intensifying geopolitical struggle. In technological terms the world is something like a single integrated system. In geopolitical terms the world is fragmenting. The instantaneous flow of information and images enabled by the internet and social media is kindling mass movements – the Arab Spring, the Orange Revolution, the Maidan events and the rise of 'people's republics' in Ukraine, among others – which serve as instruments through which the rivalries of great powers can be pursued. Touted as unifying forces, new technologies of communication are being used as weapons.

It is not hard to foresee circumstances in which the internet could fracture along the shifting lines of power. Abounding in worms and viruses that can be used to disrupt human armies and shut down vital utilities, cyberspace is a site of unceasing warfare. Partly for this reason, cyberspace could turn out to be the site of a radical evolutionary shift. We tend to think that life and mind can evolve only in forms recognizably similar to ourselves. But while they are being used as weapons, electronic technologies may also be creating a terrain on which intelligent life-forms could evolve independent of human control. Our successors may not be rebellious robots but more highly evolved descendants of computer worms. The prospect of the world being taken over by electronic viruses may seem to have evolution upside down; but that is so only if you view evolution from a human point of view.

Thinking of evolution as a succession of step-wise advances is like thinking of history as a series of incremental improvements. In each case the actuality is erratic and discontinuous. Few societies have been stable enough and resilient enough to renew themselves in recognizable forms over long stretches of time. History is littered with civilizations that have been utterly destroyed. Everywhere, the self-assured confidence of priests, scribes and intellectuals has been mocked by unexpected events, leaving all their prayers, records and treatises wholly forgotten unless they are retrieved from oblivion by future archaeologists and historians. Sudden extinction of ways of life is the human norm.

The same is true of species. Evolution has no attachment to the attributes modern thinkers imagine are essentially human – self-awareness, rationality and the like. Quite the contrary: by enabling the increase in human power that has taken place over the past few centuries, these very attributes may bring about humanity's obsolescence.

With climate systems altering as the result of human intervention, the human and the natural world are no longer separate. That does not mean humans are in control. This may be the era of the Anthropocene – the geological epoch in which human action is transforming the planet. But it is also one in which the human animal is less than ever in charge. Global warming seems to be in large part the result of the human impact on the planet, but this is not to say humans can stop the process. Whatever is done now, human expansion has triggered a shift that will persist for thousands of years. A sign of the planet healing itself, climate change will continue regardless of its impact on humankind.

There is little prospect of the human species becoming extinct in any near future. But it is difficult to imagine humans being as central in the life of the planet as they have been over the last few centuries. Humans may turn out to be like the Neanderthals, a byway in evolution. Aiming to remake the world in its own image, humankind is bringing into being a world that is post-human. However it ends, the Anthropocene will be brief.

Today's Darwinists will tell you that the task of humanity is to take charge of evolution. But 'humanity' is only a name for a ragtag animal with no capacity to take charge of anything. By destabilizing the climate, it is making the planet less hospitable to human life. By developing new technologies of mass communication and warfare, it has set in motion processes of evolution that may end up displacing it.

One way in which a post-human world could come about has been envisaged by James Lovelock, the inventor of the Gaia theory in which the planet acts, in some respects, as a single living organism. Lovelock points out that, since we know so little about how the Earth system works, we cannot remedy the disorder our expansion has inflicted on the planet:

> We can try sustainable development and renewable energy, and we can try geoengineering to help the Earth self-regulate. We can do these things with the same certainty that our eighteenth-century ancestors had about the power of mercury, arsenic or blood-letting to cure their diseases. Just as they failed utterly, so I think we also are not yet clever enough to handle the planet-sized problem and stop the Earth from over-heating.

But if humans are creating the conditions in which they cease to be the planet's dominant life-form, they may also be seeding the planet with their successors. Lovelock cites artificial intelligence and electronic life-forms as examples of human inventions that can carry on where humans leave off. Developing first as human tools, entering into symbiosis with human beings and then evolving separately from them, electronic life could develop that was more suited to thriving in the hot world human beings have created:

> We must never forget that the priceless inheritance of humans includes the know-how of electronic hardware and intelligence. The new life, if its neurons operated at electronic speed and included intelligent software, could live 1 million times faster than we do and as a result its timescale would be increased as much as a millionfold. Time enough to evolve and diversify in the same way carbon life has done. It might extend the life of Gaia still further, long enough even to enable the next Gaian dynasty, whatever that might be.

In Lovelock's premonitory vision, the Machine may sputter and stall. It will not stop. Interwoven with the life-cycle of the planet, machines have created a virtual world in which natural selection is at work at far greater speed than among the planet's biological organisms. With the rise of artificial forms of life, the next phase of evolution may already have begun.

3 Freedom for Über-marionettes

There is one kind of toy which has been on the increase for some time, and of which I have neither good nor bad to say. I refer to the scientific toy.
Charles Baudelaire, 'The Philosophy of Toys'

WHAT SCIENCE WON'T TELL YOU

In his anti-utopian novel of a fictional country *Erewhon* (an anagram of 'nowhere'), published anonymously in 1872, the Victorian novelist Samuel Butler quotes someone he describes as another writer (in fact himself), stating:

> There is no security . . . against the ultimate development of mechanical consciousness, in the fact of machines possessing little consciousness now. A mollusc has not much consciousness. Reflect upon the extraordinary advance which machines have made during the last few hundred years, and note how slowly the animal and vegetable kingdoms

> are advancing. The more highly organised machines are creatures not so much of yesterday, as of the last five minutes, so to speak, in comparison with past time. Assume for the sake of argument that conscious beings have existed for some twenty million years: see what strides machines have made in the last thousand! May not the world last twenty million years longer? If so, what will they not in the end become?

When Butler wrote this passage a century and a half ago, the idea of a conscious machine must have seemed so fantastic as to be hardly worth considering. Today there are some who expect such machines to be among us within a few decades. It would be foolish to question the increase of scientific knowledge that enables us to imagine such machines. But how will their arrival affect the way in which we think of ourselves? Will we see them as mindless mechanisms cleverly mimicking human consciousness? Or will we accept that they have something like our own self-awareness?

Whatever we decide, it will not be science that gives us the answers. It may seem curious that science can enable us to make such machines and yet be unable to tell us what it is that we have made. But science does not provide anything like a definitive picture of things. The practice of scientific investigation has gone with many different world-views. Among the scientists of the Renaissance, science and magic were closely allied. Unknown to themselves, some of the most militant twentieth-century scientific thinkers have adopted a view of things that is essentially Gnostic.

Nothing carries so much authority today as science, but there is actually no such thing as 'the scientific world-view'. Science is a method of inquiry, not a view of the world. Knowledge is growing at accelerating speed; but no advance in science will tell us whether materialism is true or false, or whether humans possess free will. The belief that the world is composed of matter is metaphysical speculation, not a testable theory. Science may succeed in explaining events in terms of causes and effects. In some accounts it may be able to formulate laws of nature. But what does it mean for something to cause something else and what is a law of nature? These are questions for philosophy or religion, not for science.

While it may be the most effective means of explaining how the world works, science cannot explain its own achievements. Scientific inquiry may be successful because everything that exists obeys a few simple laws, which humans have begun to grasp. The order of the human mind may mirror that in the cosmos. Then again, the success of science may come from the fact that its practitioners inhabit a small corner of the universe that is not chaotic. Perhaps it is the disorder of the human mind that is more reflective of reality.

How we come to have the world-views we do is an interesting question. No doubt reason plays a part, but human needs for meaning and purpose are usually more important. At times personal taste may be what decides the issue. There is nothing to say that, when all the work of reason is done, only one view of the world will remain. There may be many that fit everything that can be known. In that case you might as well choose the view of the world you find most interesting or beautiful. Adopting a world-view is more like selecting a painting to furnish a room than testing a scientific theory. The test is how it fits with your life. How does the view that humans are machines fit with our life at the present time?

Over the past few centuries, many have asserted that science shows materialism to be true and concluded that any other view of things is an illusion that must be renounced. But this modern catechism is mistaken. Even if science could show the truth of materialism, it would not follow that every other view of the world must be rejected. Quite possibly the upshot of scientific inquiry will be that the human mind cannot function without myths and fantasies. In that case science would return us to our illusions.

Whether or not materialism is true, there is no basis for the idea that humans are special in being self-aware. There is nothing uniquely human in the flicker of sentience that is commonly called consciousness. Dolphins delight in watching themselves in mirrors when they are having sex, while chimps react to the death of those they care for in much the same ways that humans do. It will be objected that these animals have no clear understanding of the kind of creature they are or what it means to die. In this regard too, however, they are no different from humans.

The idea that consciousness is a mystery is a prejudice inherited from monotheism. The early seventeenth-century French philosopher René Descartes believed that animals other than humans are insensate machines. Obviously, this was a restatement in rationalist terms of the Christian belief that only humans have souls. Even if mind and matter were categorically distinct, that would not mean humans alone have minds. It was reported that in order to test his theories, Descartes used to throw animals out of the window and observe their reactions. Looking at behaviour of this kind, one might reasonably conclude that humans are the senseless machines.

As well as believing that only humans have minds, Descartes took for granted that the mind is always aware of its own activities. This was part of the categorical distinction he made between mind and matter. But why must consciousness be all or nothing? That is not how it is in humans. Much of our lives is passed in sleep; when awake we are possessed by half-forgotten dreams. Far from the mind being always conscious of its activities, much of what the mind does goes on unknown to it.

The mystery is not consciousness but the sensations experienced by every sentient being. Whether or not a creature is self-aware, it inhabits a world it has in some measure created. No one understands how this process of creation occurs, and there is no reason to suppose anyone ever will. How the universe can encompass a possibly infinite number of subjective worlds is not obviously a soluble problem.

If we admit that consciousness comes in degrees, we will accept that the life of the spirit can flare up anywhere. Beyond humans, self-awareness may exist not only in other animals but in plants, jellyfish, worms and many other living things. The irony of materialism is that it implies exactly this. Since we know that humans are conscious, then – as Leopardi observed when he wrote of the souls of beasts – we know that other living things are conscious too. We also know the same will someday be true of machines.

Again, everyone takes for granted that if there is such a thing as free will only humans can possess it. But if consciousness can exist in many species, why not also freedom of will? Given how sadly mechanical human behaviour can be, it might be more to the point to ask whether gorillas, dolphins and other animals have free will. The idea that it could exist only in ourselves is just another example of the dogma, deriving from religion not science, which says humans are separate from the natural world.

What seems to be singularly human is not consciousness or free will but inner conflict – the contending impulses that divide us from ourselves. No other animal seeks the satisfaction of its desires and at the same time curses them as evil; spends its life terrified of death while being ready to die in order to preserve an image of itself; kills its own species for the sake of dreams. Not self-awareness but the split in the self is what makes us human.

How this split came about is unclear. There is no convincing scientific theory on the matter. The best account remains that in the book of Genesis. But the best interpretation of that unfathomably rich myth may not be the one suggested by Herr C. in Kleist's story. A version of the traditional interpretation may be truer and more subversive of current ways of thinking.

Like Herr C., modern thinkers have imagined that humans can achieve a state of freedom by eating further of the Tree of Knowledge, so that – at some point in the far future – they can become fully conscious beings. Once this has occurred, humans will be truly free. But even if such a development were possible, something would have been lost on the way. As Herr C. observed, a fully conscious marionette would be a god. It would not be human.

Those who would like to create a higher version of humanity aim to create such a marionette. Taking for granted that self-awareness is the defining attribute of human beings, they pass over the fact that many of the parts of human life that are most distinctively human have very little to do with conscious thought. We have as little idea of how we understand one another as we do of how our bodies regulate themselves. A wholly examined life – if such a life were possible – might well be wholly worthless.

Rationalists like to think the unconscious part of the mind is a relic of our animal ancestry, which further evolution will enable us to leave behind. But far more than conscious thought, it is our animal mind that makes us what we are. Science, art and human relationships emerge from processes of which we can be only dimly aware. The creative powers that are most essentially human would not necessarily be enhanced if humans were more fully conscious. Like the golems of medieval legend, a robot that possessed only conscious knowledge would be even more witless than its human creators.

Happily evolution does not work in that way. When thinking machines first arrive in the world they will be the work of flawed, intermittently lucid animals whose minds are stuffed with nonsense and delusion. In time, as Bruno Schulz perceived, matter – the true demiurge – will stir the manikins into life. From dust and dirt – 'like fate, like destiny' – the spirit will be reborn. Mutating under the pressure of entropy, the machines humans have invented will develop faults and flaws of their own. Soon they will no longer be aware of parts of their own minds; repression, denial and fantasy will cloud the empty sky of consciousness. Emerging from an inner world they cannot fathom, antagonistic impulses will govern their behaviour. Eventually these half-broken machines will have the impression that they are choosing their path through life. As in humans, this may be an illusion; but as the sensation takes hold, it will engender what in humans used to be called a soul.

ETHICS FOR PUPPETS

How is the puppet to live? You might think a puppet can have no choice in the matter. But the über-marionette – a puppet-like creature that as a result of the accidents of evolution has become self-aware – is bound to live as if it decides what it does. At times it may switch into a contemplative mode, and see its life as something that has been given to it. But when the puppet acts, it cannot help feeling that it is free.

Über-marionettes have irreducibly many divergent views of how they should live. Because these thinking puppets are in some respects everywhere the same, some values are humanly universal. Being tortured or persecuted is bad whatever the culture to which you belong, and being shown care or kindness is good. But these values are often in conflict with one another and with the particular virtues of different ways of life. Universal values do not add up to a universal morality. Unless you think human values have a source beyond the human world, you must take humans as you find them – along with their perpetually warring moralities.

At the same time some moralities are based on a more truthful rendering of the human situation than others. Taking only the western tradition, Greek ethics differs from the morality of Judaism and Christianity in a number of fundamental respects. But all three differ from the predominant forms of modern morality, and it is in these respects that these older varieties of moral thinking are most valuable.

The ancient Greeks understood ethics not as a set of commands and prohibitions but as the whole art of life. Human beings needed virtues if they were to flourish; bad states of mind and character could stand in the way of the good life. But there was no idea of evil in this Greek way of thinking. For Socrates, if you know the true nature of things you cannot help being good. The belief that human beings fail to lead the good life because of ignorance reappears in modern thinking: as scientific knowledge increases, many people now believe, so will human goodness.

In Socrates, this belief in the saving power of knowledge expressed a metaphysical faith: if a wise person was bound to be good, it was because they identified themselves with a perfect order of things that existed beyond the realm of the senses. If you read only conventional histories of philosophy, you would never know that the saint of rationalism consulted oracles, looked for meaning in dreams and obeyed an inner guide that he described as 'the voice of God'. Socrates never altogether renounced ancient Greek shamanism; but his intimations went far beyond such beliefs and practices. Claiming he knew nothing for sure, he never doubted that the world was rational. Lying at the bottom of the Socratic faith in reason is a mystical equation of the true and the good. Its origins forgotten or denied, this became the basis of western rationalism – the hollowed-out version of Socrates' teaching that Nietzsche mockingly called Socratism.

Happily there was more to ancient Greece than

philosophy. The Greek tragedians expressed a more truthful version of human experience: no amount of virtue or reasoning can ensure that human beings live a worthwhile life. Greek myth tells the same story. Having formed humans from clay, Prometheus gives them an upright stance and the use of fire. Zeus punishes Prometheus by binding him to a rock, where he is chained everlastingly in a life without sleep or any rest from torment. Even the self-assertion of a god ends in hubris, which is always punished.

Judaism contains something akin to the Greek sense of tragedy: despite the fact that he ended by accepting God's will, Job's questioning of divine justice posed a challenge to any belief in ultimate moral harmony. In contrast, by affirming that God can redeem any evil and even annul death, Christianity shows that it is an anti-tragic faith. If Jesus had died on the cross and stayed dead, that would have been a tragedy. In the Christian story, however, he was resurrected and came back into the world. Yet Christianity is still closer to ancient understandings of tragedy than it is to modern ways of thinking. As developed by Paul and Augustine, Christianity recognized that nothing humans can do will raise them from their fallen state. Here Christians are not so different from the ancient Greeks, who knew that nothing can protect humans from fate.

Where these older moralities are superior to modern

moralities is in understanding that humankind can never overcome its inherent limitations. It is only in recent times that human beings have come to see themselves as potentially godlike. Ancient thinkers were more intelligent as well as more honest. They knew that human action can change the world, sometimes for the good. They also knew that civilizations rise and fall; what has been gained will be lost, regained and then lost again in a cycle as natural as the seasons.

This view of things was articulated in a letter of Octavius Caesar, otherwise known as the founder of the Roman Empire Augustus, written when he was travelling by sea in AD 14:

> Rome is not eternal; it does not matter. Rome will fall; it does not matter. The barbarian will conquer; it does not matter. There was a moment of Rome, and it will not wholly die; the barbarian will become the Rome he conquers; the language will smooth his rough tongue; the vision of what he destroys will flow in his blood. And in time that is as ceaseless as this salt sea upon which I am so frailly suspended, the cost is nothing, is less than nothing.

Today practically no one could accept such a stoical ethic. The letter is fiction – a passage in John

Williams's novel *Augustus*, first published in 1972. Yet there can be little doubt that attitudes like those of Augustus were common in the ancient world. The *Meditations* of Marcus Aurelius, a record of the thoughts of a Roman emperor who lived and ruled a hundred years after Augustus, contains many similar expressions of Stoic philosophy. Like the author of the fictional letter, Aurelius urges that civilization must be resolutely defended against barbarism without any hope that civilization can finally prevail.

Living before the triumph of Christianity, Augustus and Aurelius did not imagine that history had any overall meaning. There was no hidden thread of redemption or improvement in the passage of events. Reared on a curdled brew of Socratism and scraps of decayed Christianity, modern thinkers condemn this as a counsel of despair. In the ancient world it expressed health and clarity of mind. If that sanity cannot now be recovered, it is because the monotheistic faith that history has meaning continues to shape the modern way of thinking even after monotheism itself has been rejected. The most radical modern critic of religion, Nietzsche lamented monotheism's formative influence while exhibiting its influence himself. The absurd figure of the *Übermensch* embodies the fantasy that history can be given meaning by the force of human will. Aiming in his early work to restore the sense of tragedy, Nietzsche ended up promoting yet another version of the modern project of human self-assertion.

If you want to reject any idea of God, you must accept that 'humanity' – the universal subject that finds redemption in history – also does not exist. That few can do this is one reason why the ethics of ancient times are irretrievable. But there is another: defending civilization is intractably difficult work, while barbarism comes with a promise of transgression and excitement. The fragility of civilization is testimony to the perennial dream of a life without restraint.

Before it means anything else, civilization implies restraint in the use of force; but when it serves noble-sounding goals, violence has a glamour that is irresistible. Like the Aztecs, modern humankind is wedded to killing; but the visions with which it justifies mass slaughter are more primitive and unreal than the Aztecs' mocking gods. Wars and revolutions launched for the sake of universal freedom have demanded human sacrifice on a scale the Aztecs could not have imagined. What Leopardi called 'the barbarism of reason' has proved to be more savage than the barbarism of the past.

Freedom among humans is not a natural human condition. It is the practice of mutual non-interference – a rare skill that is slowly learnt and quickly forgotten. The purpose of this 'negative' freedom is not to promote the evolution of humans into rational beings or to enable them to govern themselves; it is to protect human beings from each other. Divided against itself, the human animal is unnaturally violent by its very nature. The old-fashioned freedom of non-interference accepts this fact. For that very reason, this freedom is bound to be devalued in a time when any reference to the flaws of the human animal is condemned as blasphemy.

At present the practices in which this freedom has been embodied – habeas corpus, open courts, the rule of law – are being compromised or else junked. Torture has been adopted, along with kidnap and secret rendition, as an essential weapon in the struggle for human rights. The only safeguards of freedom that have ever been halfway effective are being cast aside in the pursuit of figments. At the same time new varieties of despotism are emerging in many parts of the world. Contemporary governments are deploying the latest technologies to develop hyper-modern techniques of control far more invasive than those of traditional tyrannies.

If freedom of any kind can be found in these conditions, it is some version of the inward variety that was prized by the thinkers of the ancient world. In some future turn of the cycle, freedom in the relations of humans with one another may return; but for the present and the future that can be clearly foreseen, it is only the freedom that can be realized within each human being that can be secure.

Nothing is more alien to the spirit of the age than to suggest that anyone might seek inner freedom, for it suggests doubt as to the prevailing faith that the human world is improving. Clearly, there are many who cannot do without this comforting faith. The most charitable course is to leave them to their slumbers. But for those of a more venturesome turn of mind, it may be worth considering – if only as a thought-experiment – what inner freedom might mean today.

GRAVITY AND THE FALL

As Herr C. portrays them, marionettes have an advantage over humans: the puppets can defy gravity. Recall his rhapsodic description: 'these puppets have the advantage of being *resistant to gravity*. Of the heaviness of matter, the factor that most works against the dancer, they are entirely ignorant: because the force lifting them into the air is greater than the one attaching them to the earth . . .' The marionette is able to resist gravity because it does not have to decide how it will live. Humans are fumbling in their movements, and forever on the point of falling down. But what of the über-marionette – the human being that knows it is a machine? Must it envy the graceful automatism of the puppet?

In the story told by Herr C., human beings become free when they become fully conscious. For these godlike creatures, there can be nothing that is mysterious. Mystery fades away with ever greater conscious awareness, and true freedom means living by that inner light. This is, of course, a very old faith – the faith of the Gnostics, and also of Socrates. Both believed that freedom was achieved by the possession of a special kind of knowledge. Modern rationalism is another version of this religion. Contemporary evangelists for evolution, trans-humanists and techno-futurists are also followers of this creed. All of them promote the project of expelling mystery from the mind.

The trouble with this project is that it has the effect of confining the mind within itself. In a world where there is nothing that cannot be explained, everything that happens fits into a hidden scheme. In Gnosticism, the world is the plaything of a demiurge. For conspiracy theorists, history is scripted by occult agencies. For secular rationalists, enlightenment is thwarted by the sinister forces of superstition and reaction. There is a pattern here: if you aim to exorcize mystery from your mind, you end up – like Philip K. Dick – locked in a paranoid universe and possessed by demons.

From being seemingly annihilated by Christianity, Gnosticism has conquered the world. Belief in the liberating power of knowledge has become the ruling illusion of modern humankind. Most want to believe that some kind of explanation or understanding will deliver them from their conflicts. Yet being divided from yourself goes with being self-aware. This is the truth in the Genesis myth: the Fall is not an event at the beginning of history but the intrinsic condition of self-conscious beings.

Only creatures that are as flawed and ignorant as humans can be free in the way humans are free. We do not know how matter came to dream our world into being; we do not know what, if anything, comes when the dream ends for us and we die. We yearn for a type of knowledge that would make us other than we are – though what we would like to be, we cannot say. Why try to escape from yourself? Accepting the fact of unknowing makes possible an inner freedom very different from that pursued by Gnostics. If you have this negative capability, you will not want a higher form of consciousness; your ordinary mind will give you all you need. Rather than trying to impose sense on your life, you will be content to let meaning come and go. Instead of becoming an unfaltering puppet, you will make your way in the stumbling human world. Über-marionettes do not have to wait until they can fly before they can be free. Not looking to ascend into the heavens, they can find freedom in falling to earth.

Acknowledgements

I have been exceptionally fortunate in the help I have received in writing this book. Simon Winder, my editor at Penguin, is everything an editor should be and more; his comments have improved the book immeasurably. Eric Chinski, my editor at Farrar, Straus & Giroux in the US, has given me and the book immense support and encouragement. My friend Adam Phillips has given invaluable advice, which helped give the book the shape I had dimly in mind. My agent Tracy Bohan has given me all that a writer could ask; throughout the book's gestation she has been unfailingly supportive and encouraging. Her colleague at the Wylie Agency Catrin Evans looked after me while Tracy was on maternity leave, making the book's completion smooth and problem-free.

Conversations with a number of people stirred the thoughts that went into the book. Among those I would like to thank are Bryan Appleyard, Bas Heijne,

David Herman, Gerard Lemos, James Lovelock, David Rieff, Paul Schütze, Will Self, John Simenon, Geoffrey Smith, Marcel Theroux and Nassim Taleb.

I have used the lines from R. S. Thomas's poem 'The Refusal' as the epigraph for Chapter 2 with permission from Bloodaxe Books and the Estate of R. S. Thomas.

Since I have not always taken the advice I was given, it is important to note that responsibility for the book remains mine. The same applies to the use I have made of the writers and books I have cited.

As always, my greatest debt is to my wife Mieko.

John Gray

Notes

EPIGRAPHS

p. v 'a marionette or in a god': Heinrich von Kleist, 'The Puppet Theatre', *Selected Writings*, ed. and trans. David Constantine, Indianapolis/Cambridge, Hackett Publishing, 2004, 416.
p. v 'made out of dust': Philip K. Dick, *The Three Stigmata of Palmer Eldritch*, London, Gollancz, 2003, epigraph.

CHAPTER 1: THE FAITH OF PUPPETS

p. 1 'their possible victory': J. L. Borges, 'A Defense of Basilides the False', *The Total Library*, London, Penguin Books, 2001, 68.
pp. 2–5 'history of the world': Heinrich von Kleist, 'The Puppet Theatre', *Selected Writings*, ed. and trans. David Constantine, Indianapolis/Cambridge, Hackett Publishing, 2004, 411–16.
p. 10 'in modern science and politics': I consider the

influence of Gnostic thinking on modern politics in *Black Mass: Apocalyptic Religion and the Death of Utopia*, London, Penguin Books, 2007, 15–16, 95–6.

pp. 12–13 'each other's prey . . .': Lawrence Durrell, *The Avignon Quintet*, London, Faber & Faber, 2004, 134–5.

pp. 14–15 'entirely into light': For a discussion of Bernal and the passage from his book, see Philip Ball, *Unnatural: The Heretical Idea of Making People*, London, Bodley Head, 2011, 171–2.

p. 15 The subtitle of Kurzweil's book: Ray Kurzweil, *The Singularity is Near: When Humans Transcend Biology*, London, Penguin Books, 2005.

p. 15 two articles of faith: The best account of Gnosticism is that of Hans Jonas, *The Gnostic Religion: The Message of the Alien God and the Beginnings of Christianity*, 2nd edn, Boston, Beacon Press, 1963. See also Giovanni Filoramo, *A History of Gnosticism*, trans. Anthony Alcock, Cambridge, Mass. and Oxford, Blackwell, 1992.

p. 16 originated with Zoroaster: For an illuminating study of the idea of evil in western religion, see Yuri Stoyanov, *The Other God: Dualist Religions from Antiquity to the Cathar Heresy*, New Haven and London, Yale University Press, 2000.

pp. 17–18 'bring forth good fruit': For these quotes, see Stoyanov, *The Other God*, 2.

p. 18 'Truth and Untruth': Ibid., 33.

p. 20 'dreams up within itself': Bruno Schulz, *The Street of Crocodiles and Other Stories*, trans. Celina Wieniewska, London, Penguin Books, 2008, 31.

pp. 20–21 'in one word – Demiurgy': Ibid., 33.
pp. 21–2 'no more than a parody?': Ibid., 35.
p. 22 'semblance of a tailors' dummy': Ibid., 33.
p. 22–3 'heretical and criminal methods': Ibid., 32.
p. 23 'mutilated, denatured mythology': Schulz, 'The Mythicization of Reality', quoted by David A. Goldfarb, Introduction to ibid., xv.
p. 28 'complete in itself': *Zibaldone: The Notebooks of Leopardi*, ed. Michael Caesar and Franco D'Intino, London, Penguin Books, 2013, 1819.
p. 29 'harmful to it': Ibid., 207.
pp. 29–30 'people to savagery': Ibid., 23–4.
p. 31 'our thought corporeally': Ibid., 1913.
p. 31 'than after it': Ibid., 248.
p. 32 'like Freud, a hundred years later': I discuss Freud's reasons for denying that Christianity was an advance on Judaism in *The Silence of Animals: On Progress and Other Modern Myths*, London, Penguin Books, 2013, 103.
p. 32 'that of antiquity': *Zibaldone*, 80.
p. 32 'expressions of "half-philosophy"': Ibid., 285.
p. 33 'present-day human life': Ibid., 876.
p. 34 'sinking in this sea': Giacomo Leopardi, *The Canti, with a Selection of his Prose*, trans. J. G. Nichols, Manchester, Carcanet, 1998, 53.
pp. 34–5 'free from suffering': Ibid., 101–2.
p. 35 'evil is *necessary*?': *Zibaldone*, 2059.
p. 36 'of living beings': Ibid., 1997–8.
p. 37 'all our ills': Leopardi, *The Canti*, 139.
p. 37 'his feeble will': *The Short Fiction of Edgar Allan*

Poe, ed. Stuart Levine and Susan Levine, Urbana and Chicago, University of Illinois Press, 1990, 79.
p. 38 'their being otherwise': Joseph Glanvill, *Scepsis Scientifica*, quoted in H. Stanley Redgrove and I. M. L. Redgrove, *Joseph Glanvill and Psychical Research in the Seventeenth Century*, London, William Rider, 1921, 32–3.
p. 39 'well of Democritus': *Short Fiction*, 40.
pp. 39–40 'man and God': Ibid., 10–11.
p. 40 'rushing towards him': Peter Ackroyd, *Poe: A Life Cut Short*, London, Vintage Books, 2009, p. 159.
p. 42 '(I believe) other dreams': Jorge Luis Borges, 'When Fiction Lives in Fiction', *The Total Library*, 162.
p. 43 'insert him into reality': J. L. Borges, 'The Circular Ruins', *Fictions*, London, Penguin Books, 1970, 73.
p. 43 'the faceless wind': Ibid., 74.
p. 44 'dreamt by another': Ibid., 77.
pp. 45–6 'of other worlds': Stanislav Lem, *Solaris, The Chain of Chance, A Perfect Vacuum*, London, Penguin Books, 1985, 75–6.
pp. 47–8 'was not past': Ibid., 194–5.
p. 49 'does not remember': Philip K. Dick, *The Shifting Realities of Philip K. Dick: Selected Literary and Philosophical Writings*, ed. and introduced by Lawrence Sutin, New York, Vintage Books, 1995, 294.
p. 50 'to be thawed out': Ibid., 216.
p. 51 'human being at all': Lawrence Sutin, *Divine Invasions: A Life of Philip K. Dick*, London, Gollancz, 2006, 14.

p. 51 'it was God': Ibid., 127.
p. 51 'in the sky': Ibid., 128.
p. 53 'full-blown paranoia': For a detailed account of Dick's breakdown, see ibid., 210.
pp. 55–6 'a Linda Ronstadt obsession': *The Exegesis of Philip K. Dick*, ed. Pamela Jackson and Jonathan Lethem, London, Gollancz, 2011, 895.
p. 57 'benign proto-entity': Dick, *Shifting Realities*, 284.
p. 58 'our own view': Ibid., 214.
p. 58 'creation is visible': Quoted in Sutin, *Divine Invasions*, 229.
p. 61 'was never written': Ibid., 266.
p. 61 'unconscious messenger to conscious': *Exegesis*, 423–4.
p. 61 not 'mere faith': Sutin, *Divine Invasions*, 283.
pp. 63–4 'from another meadow . . .': Arkady and Boris Strugatsky, *Roadside Picnic*, trans. Olena Bormashenko, London, Gollancz, 2012, 131–2.
p. 64 'chivalry and generosity': Ibid., 196–7.
p. 65 'nothing upsets it': Ibid., 128.
pp. 66–7 'enemy to man': T. F. Powys, *Unclay*, Sherborne, Sundial Press, 2011, 275.
p. 67 'a road to God': Theodore Francis Powys, *Soliloquies of a Hermit*, London, Village Press, 1975, 1.
p. 68 'existence in fact': T. F. Powys, *Mr Weston's Good Wine*, London, Penguin Books, 1937, 26.
p. 69 'the firm will end': Ibid. 173–4.
pp. 69–70 'Mr Weston was gone': Ibid., 239.

p. 71 'to everlasting death': T. F. Powys, *The Only Penitent*, London, Chatto & Windus, 1931, 56–7.
p. 72 'our old immortality': Powys, *Soliloquies of a Hermit*, 90.

CHAPTER 2: IN THE PUPPET THEATRE

p. 73 'he was no angel': R. S. Thomas, 'The Refusal', *Selected Poems*, London, Penguin Books, 2004, 247.
p. 73 'the Florentine Codex': Inga Clendinnen, *Aztecs: An Interpretation*, Cambridge, Cambridge University Press, 1991,141.
pp. 74–5 'regard for beauty': Clendinnen, *Aztecs*, 2
p. 76 'well-swept paths': Ibid., 16.
pp. 76–7 'held in check': Ibid., 53–4.
p. 77 'celebrated in verse': See *Flower and Song: Poems of the Aztec Peoples*, trans. and ed. Edward Kissam and Michael Schmidt, London, Anvil Press Poetry, 2009, 97–116.
pp. 77–8 'pulse of living': Clendinnen, *Aztecs*, 88.
p. 79 'of violent death . . .': Thomas Hobbes, *Leviathan*, London, J. M. Dent, 1914, 66, 64–5.
p. 81 'am the enemy': 'Tezcatlipoca's Song', in *Flower and Song*, 94.
p. 82 'and our enemy': Clendinnen, *Aztecs*, 80,
p. 83 'to be demonstrated': Ibid., 3.
p. 83 'from their mothers': Ibid., 88.
p. 84 'my very self?': Ibid., 95.
p. 85 'the temple walls': Ibid., 261.

pp. 85–6 'conditions of existence': Ibid., 262–3.
p. 88 'but man only': Hobbes, *Leviathan*, 20.
p. 89 'is left standing': Clendinnen, *Aztecs*, 17.
p. 91 'a popular message': See Steven Pinker, *The Better Angels of our Nature: Why Violence has Declined*, London, Penguin Books, 2012.
p. 94 'taking them too seriously': For a critical assessment of Pinker's use of battlefield statistics, see John Arquilla, 'The Big Kill', *Foreign Policy*, 3 December 2012. For a methodological critique of Pinker's use of statistics, see Nassim Taleb, 'The Pinker Problem', Nassim Nicholas Taleb's web page, www.fooledbyrandomness.com.
p. 95 'numbers of fatalities': See Edward Wilson, 'Thank you, Vasili Arkhipov, the man who stopped nuclear war', *Guardian*, 27 October 2012.
p. 97 'mingled with angelology': Frances Yates, *The Rosicrucian Enlightenment*, London, Routledge, 2008, xiii.
p. 98 'revolved around humans': Benjamin Woolley, *The Queen's Conjuror: The Life and Magic of Dr Dee*, London, Flamingo, 2002, 328.
p. 102 'exorcised it . . .': Norbert Wiener, *The Human Use of Human Beings*, 2nd edn, New York, Doubleday, 1954, 34–5. This passage from Wiener is quoted in Philip Mirowski, *Machine Dreams: Economics Becomes a Cyborg Science*, Cambridge, Cambridge University Press, 2002, 55–6.
p. 103 'as a variation?': Norbert Wiener, *God and Golem, Inc.: A Comment on Certain Points Where Cybernetics Impinges on Religion*, Cambridge, Mass., MIT Press, 1964, 29.

p. 104 'automaton will be': Quoted in Mirowski, *Machine Dreams*, 149.
p. 104 'human-machine civilization': John von Neumann, *The Computer and the Brain*, New Haven and London, Yale University Press, 2012, Foreword by Ray Kurzweil, xi–xii. Kurzweil has developed his views in *How to Create a Mind: The Secret of Human Thought Revealed*, London, Duckworth, 2014. I have assessed Kurzweil's views, and suggested that they express a modern type of Gnosticism, in *The Immortalization Commission: The Strange Quest to Defeat Death*, London, Penguin Books, 2012, 217–18.
p. 106 'acquired nuclear weapons': Mirowski, *Machine Dreams*, 167.
p. 106 'and their implications': Ibid., 19.
p. 107 'in the machine': Ellen Ullman, quoted in ibid., 232.
p. 108 'during the Second World War': For an illuminating account of Turing's achievements and tragic life, see Andrew Hodges, *Alan Turing: The Enigma*, London, Vintage Books, 1992.
p. 109 'flirting with their users': See Nadia Khomani, '2029: the year when computers will outsmart their makers', *Guardian*, 22 February 2014, for an interview with Kurzweil in which he makes these predictions.
p. 110 'societies are constructed': Leonard C. Lewin, *Report from Iron Mountain: On the Possibility and Desirability of Peace*, New York, Free Press, 1996, 93.
pp. 110–11 'unskilled labor supply': Ibid., 56–7.
p. 111–12 'circumstances of historical relationship': Ibid., 105.

p. 113 '*New York Times*': Lewin (1916–99) was also the author of *Triage*, New York, Warner Communications, 1973, a dystopian novel about covert government programmes designed to eliminate groups judged to be socially unfit.
p. 116 'kind of stardom': Guy Debord, *Comments on the Society of the Spectacle*, trans. Malcolm Imrie, London, Verso, 1990, 10–11.
p. 117 'left a mark': For a reference to Debord's disciple working for Berlusconi, see Andrew Hussey, 'From Being to Nothingness', *Independent*, 10 December 1995.
p. 118 'an eternal present': Debord, *Comments on the Society of the Spectacle*, 11–12.
p. 119 'great French intellectuals': Andrew Gallix, 'The resurrection of Guy Debord', *Guardian*, 18 March 2009.
p. 119 'whose existence it denies . . .': Debord, *Comments on the Society of the Spectacle*, 52.
p. 121 'an impossible dream': I discussed the rise of the surveillance state in my book *Al Qaeda and What It Means to be Modern*, London, Faber & Faber, 2003, 83–4.
p. 127 'without altering anything?': Leonardo Sciascia, *The Moro Affair*, London, Granta Books, 2002, 24–5.
p. 129 'is left open': Philip Willan, *Puppetmasters: The Political Use of Terrorism in Italy*, San José, New York, Lincoln and Shanghai, Authors Choice Press, 2002, 156–7.
p. 131 'question of "public order"': Gianfranco Sanguinetti, *On Terrorism and the State: The Theory and Practice of Terrorism Divulged for the First Time*, London, B. M. Chronos, 1982, 59.

p. 133 'directed by the state': For discussion of Sanguinetti's views and changes of mind, see ibid., Foreword to the English edition by Lucy Forsyth, 10–11, and Andrew Hussey, *The Game of War: The Life and Death of Guy Debord*, London, Pimlico, 2001, 310–21.
p. 134 'twentieth-century history': Norman Cohn, *Warrant for Genocide: The Myth of the Jewish World Conspiracy and the Protocols of the Elders of Zion*, London, Serif, 1996, 117.
p. 135 'factions in the CIA': Richard H. Popkin, *The Second Oswald*, Raleigh, NC, C&M Online Media, 2006, 87–9.
p. 136 'at this point': Ibid., 89.
pp. 137–8 'of her cell': E. M. Forster, 'The Machine Stops', in *Selected Stories*, ed. with an Introduction and Notes by David Leavitt and Mark Mitchell, London, Penguin Books, 2001, 121.
pp. 138–41 'generations who have gone': Ibid., 94, 98, 100, 101, 104, 116, 120, 121.
p. 145 'from over-heating': James Lovelock, *A Rough Ride to the Future*, London, Allen Lane, 2014, 150–51.
p. 146 'whatever that might be': Ibid., 161.

CHAPTER 3: FREEDOM FOR ÜBER-MARIONETTES

p. 147 'the scientific toy': Charles Baudelaire, 'The Philosophy of Toys', in *On Dolls*, ed. Kenneth Gross, London, Notting Hill Editions, 2013, 17.

pp. 147–8 'in the end become?': Samuel Butler, 'The Book of the Machines', *Erewhon*, ed. with an Introduction by Peter Mudford, London, Penguin Books, 1985, p. 199.

p. 157 'the voice of God': For Socrates' faith in oracles and dreams in the context of ancient Greek shamanism, see E. R. Dodds, *The Greeks and the Irrational*, Berkeley and London, University of California Press, 1951, 184–5. I discussed Socrates' debts to shamanism in *Straw Dogs: Thoughts on Humans and Other Animals*, London, Granta Books, 2003, 25–6.

p. 157 'mockingly called Socratism': For Nietzsche on Socrates, see Friedrich Nietzsche, *The Birth of Tragedy*, trans. Shaun Whiteside, London, Penguin Books, 2003, pp. 64–75.

p. 159 'less than nothing': John Williams, *Augustus*, Vintage Books, London, 2003, 310.

p. 163 'to the earth . . .': Heinrich von Kleist, 'The Puppet Theatre', *Selected Writings*, ed. and trans. David Constantine, Indianapolis/Cambridge, Hackett Publishing, 2004, 414.

ALLEN LANE

an imprint of

PENGUIN BOOKS

Recently Published

Peter H. Wilson, *The Holy Roman Empire: A Thousand Years of Europe's History*

Todd Rose, *The End of Average: How to Succeed in a World that Values Sameness*

Frank Trentmann, *Empire of Things: How We Became a World of Consumers, from the Fifteenth Century to the Twenty-First*

Laura Ashe, *Richard II: A Brittle Glory*

John Donvan and Caren Zucker, *In a Different Key: The Story of Autism*

Jack Shenker, *The Egyptians: A Radical Story*

Tim Judah, *In Wartime: Stories from Ukraine*

Serhii Plokhy, *The Gates of Europe: A History of Ukraine*

Robin Lane Fox, *Augustine: Conversions and Confessions*

Peter Hennessy and James Jinks, *The Silent Deep: The Royal Navy Submarine Service Since 1945*

Sean McMeekin, *The Ottoman Endgame: War, Revolution and the Making of the Modern Middle East, 1908–1923*

Charles Moore, *Margaret Thatcher: The Authorized Biography, Volume Two: Everything She Wants*

Dominic Sandbrook, *The Great British Dream Factory: The Strange History of Our National Imagination*

Larissa MacFarquhar, *Strangers Drowning: Voyages to the Brink of Moral Extremity*

Niall Ferguson, *Kissinger: 1923-1968: The Idealist*

Carlo Rovelli, *Seven Brief Lessons on Physics*

Tim Blanning, *Frederick the Great: King of Prussia*

Ian Kershaw, *To Hell and Back: Europe, 1914–1949*

Pedro Domingos, *The Master Algorithm: How the Quest for the Ultimate Learning Machine Will Remake Our World*

David Wootton, *The Invention of Science: A New History of the Scientific Revolution*

Christopher Tyerman, *How to Plan a Crusade: Reason and Religious War in the Middle Ages*

Andy Beckett, *Promised You A Miracle: UK 80–82*

Carl Watkins, *Stephen: The Reign of Anarchy*

Anne Curry, *Henry V: From Playboy Prince to Warrior King*

John Gillingham, *William II: The Red King*

Roger Knight, *William IV: A King at Sea*

Douglas Hurd, *Elizabeth II: The Steadfast*

Richard Nisbett, *Mindware: Tools for Smart Thinking*

Jochen Bleicken, *Augustus: The Biography*

Paul Mason, *PostCapitalism: A Guide to Our Future*

Frank Wilczek, *A Beautiful Question: Finding Nature's Deep Design*

Roberto Saviano, *Zero Zero Zero*

Owen Hatherley, *Landscapes of Communism: A History Through Buildings*

César Hidalgo, *Why Information Grows: The Evolution of Order, from Atoms to Economies*

Aziz Ansari and Eric Klinenberg, *Modern Romance: An Investigation*

Sudhir Hazareesingh, *How the French Think: An Affectionate Portrait of an Intellectual People*

Steven D. Levitt and Stephen J. Dubner, *When to Rob a Bank: A Rogue Economist's Guide to the World*

Leonard Mlodinow, *The Upright Thinkers: The Human Journey from Living in Trees to Understanding the Cosmos*

Hans Ulrich Obrist, *Lives of the Artists, Lives of the Architects*

Richard H. Thaler, *Misbehaving: The Making of Behavioural Economics*

Sheldon Solomon, Jeff Greenberg and Tom Pyszczynski, *Worm at the Core: On the Role of Death in Life*

Nathaniel Popper, *Digital Gold: The Untold Story of Bitcoin*

Dominic Lieven, *Towards the Flame: Empire, War and the End of Tsarist Russia*

Noel Malcolm, *Agents of Empire: Knights, Corsairs, Jesuits and Spies in the Sixteenth-Century Mediterranean World*

James Rebanks, *The Shepherd's Life: A Tale of the Lake District*

David Brooks, *The Road to Character*

Joseph Stiglitz, *The Great Divide*

Ken Robinson and Lou Aronica, *Creative Schools: Revolutionizing Education from the Ground Up*

Clotaire Rapaille and Andrés Roemer, *Move UP: Why Some Cultures Advances While Others Don't*

Jonathan Keates, *William III and Mary II: Partners in Revolution*

David Womersley, *James II: The Last Catholic King*

Richard Barber, *Henry II: A Prince Among Princes*

Jane Ridley, *Victoria: Queen, Matriarch, Empress*

John Gray, *The Soul of the Marionette: A Short Enquiry into Human Freedom*

Emily Wilson, *Seneca: A Life*

Michael Barber, *How to Run a Government: So That Citizens Benefit and Taxpayers Don't Go Crazy*

Dana Thomas, *Gods and Kings: The Rise and Fall of Alexander McQueen and John Galliano*

Steven Weinberg, *To Explain the World: The Discovery of Modern Science*

Jennifer Jacquet, *Is Shame Necessary?: New Uses for an Old Tool*

Eugene Rogan, *The Fall of the Ottomans: The Great War in the Middle East, 1914-1920*

Norman Doidge, *The Brain's Way of Healing: Stories of Remarkable Recoveries and Discoveries*

John Hooper, *The Italians*

Sven Beckert, *Empire of Cotton: A New History of Global Capitalism*

Mark Kishlansky, *Charles I: An Abbreviated Life*

Philip Ziegler, *George VI: The Dutiful King*

David Cannadine, *George V: The Unexpected King*

Stephen Alford, *Edward VI: The Last Boy King*